Songs of Ourselves

The University of Cambridge International Examinations
Anthology of Poetry in English

Delhi • Bangalore • Mumbai • Kolkata • Chennai • Hyderabad • Pune

Published by
Cambridge University Press India Pvt. Ltd.
under the Foundation Books imprint
CAMBRIDGE HOUSE
4381/4, Ansari Road, Daryaganj
New Delhi - 110 002

- C-22, C-Block, Brigade M.M., K.R. Road, Jayanagar, **Bangalore** 560 070
- Plot No. 80, Service Industries, Shirvane, Sector-1, Nerul, **Navi Mumbai** 400 706
- 10, Raja Subodh Mullick Square, 2nd Floor, **Kolkata** 700 013
- 21/1 (New No. 49), 1st Floor, Model School Road, Thousand Lights, **Chennai** 600 006
- House No. 3-5-874/6/4, (Near Apollo Hospital), Hyderguda, **Hyderabad** 500 029
- Agarwal Pride, 'A' Wing, 1308 Kasba Peth, Near Surya Hospital, **Pune** 411 011

© University of Cambridge Local Examinations Syndicate
First Published 2005
First Reprint 2006 (twice), 2007 (twice), 2008, 2009 (twice), 2010, 2011 (twice) 2012

ISBN 10: 81-7596-248-8 (Paperback)
ISBN 13: 978-81-7596-248-4 (Paperback)

Published by Manas Saikia for Cambridge University Press India Pvt. Ltd. and typeset in
Replika Press Pvt. Ltd. and Printed at Sanat Printers, Kundli, Haryana, India.

Contents

Introduction   *xiii*
Acknowledgements   *xv*

PART 1

Poems from the Sixteenth and Early Seventeenth Centuries

1   Song: *Why So Pale and Wan, Fond Lover?*   3
    SIR JOHN SUCKLING
2   *What Thing Is Love?*   4
    GEORGE PEELE
3   *Sonnet 11*   5
    LADY MARY WROTH
4   Song: *Sigh No More, Ladies*   6
    WILLIAM SHAKESPEARE
5   Song: *Weep You No More, Sad Fountains*   7
    ANONYMOUS
6   *When I Was Fair And Young*   8
    QUEEN ELIZABETH I
7   *They Flee From Me, That Sometime Did Me Seek*   9
    SIR THOMAS WYATT
8   *Sonnet 61*   10
    MICHAEL DRAYTON
9   Song: *Go, Lovely Rose!*   11
    EDMUND WALLER
10 *No Crooked Leg, No Bleared Eye*   12
    QUEEN ELIZABETH I
11 *Sonnet 31*   13
    SIR PHILIP SIDNEY
12 *Written The Night Before His Execution*   14
    CHIDIOCK TICHBOURNE
13 *The Author's Epitaph, Made By Himself*   15
    SIR WALTER RALEIGH
14 *A Litany In Time Of Plague*   16
    THOMAS NASHE
15 *Sonnet 19*   18
    LADY MARY WROTH
16 From *Underwoods*   19
    BEN JONSON

17   Song: *Fear No More The Heat O' Th' Sun*   20
     WILLIAM SHAKESPEARE
18   *A Song*   22
     THOMAS CAREW
19   *Walsingham*   23
     SIR WALTER RALEIGH
20   *The Flowers That on The Banks and Walks Did Grow*   25
     AEMILIA LANYER
21   *Come Live with me, and be my Love*   27
     CHRISTOPHER MARLOWE
22   *Sonnet 54*   28
     EDMUND SPENSER
23   *What is Our Life?*   29
     SIR WALTER RALEIGH
24   *Sonnet 75*   30
     EDMUND SPENSER
25   Song: *Spring, The Sweet Spring*   31
     THOMAS NASHE
26   *Sonnet 18*   32
     WILLIAM SHAKESPEARE
27   *Sonnet 73*   33
     WILLIAM SHAKESPEARE
28   Song: *Blow, Blow, Thou Winter Wind*   34
     WILLIAM SHAKESPEARE
29   *The Procession of The Seasons*   35
     EDMUND SPENSER
30   *The Man of Life Upright*   37
     THOMAS CAMPION
31   *A Mind Content*   38
     ROBERT GREENE
32   *I Grieve, and Dare Not Show my Discontent*   39
     QUEEN ELIZABETH I
33   Song: *To Celia*   40
     BEN JONSON
34   *Golden Slumbers*   41
     THOMAS DEKKER
35   Song: *Full Fathom Five*   42
     WILLIAM SHAKESPEARE
36   *A Farewell To The Reader*   43
     ISABELLA WHITNEY

PART 2

Poems from the Seventeenth and Eighteenth Centuries

37 *The Fly*   47
WILLIAM BLAKE

38 *Shadows In The Water*   48
THOMAS TRAHERNE

39 *Ants* (From *Dryades*)   51
WILLIAM DIAPER

40 *The Ant or Emmet*   52
ISAAC WATTS

41 *The Grasshopper*   53
ABRAHAM COWLEY

42 *To The Virgins, To Make Much of Time*   55
ROBERT HERRICK

43 *The Call*   56
JOHN HALL

44 *Love*   58
HENRY BAKER

45 Song: *Love Armed*   60
APHRA BEHN

46 Song: *I Feed A Flame Within*   61
JOHN DRYDEN

47 *The Mower To The Glow-Worms*   62
ANDREW MARVELL

48 *Her Window*   63
RICHARD LEIGH

49 *To One That Asked Me Why I Loved J.G.*   65
'EPHELIA'

50 *As Loving Hind That, Hartless, Wants Her Deer*   67
ANNE BRADSTREET

51 *A Married State*   69
KATHERINE PHILIPS

52 *Ode on Solitude*   70
ALEXANDER POPE

53 From *A Dialogue Between a Squeamish Cotting Mechanic and His
    Sluttish Wife, In a Kitchen*   71
EDWARD WARD

54 From *On My Dreaming of my Wife*   74
JONATHAN RICHARDSON

55 *William and Margaret*   75
DAVID MALLET

56 *The Widow*   78
ROBERT SOUTHEY

57   *The Rights of Woman*   80
     ANNA LAETITIA BARBAULD

58   Song: *To Lucasta, Going to The Wars*   82
     RICHARD LOVELACE

59   *Ode: I Hate That Drum's Discordant Sound*   83
     JOHN SCOTT

60   From *Blenheim*   84
     JOHN PHILIPS

61   *The Hunting of The Hare*   86
     MARGARET CAVENDISH, DUCHESS OF NEWCASTLE

62   From *A Satyr Against Mankind*   90
     JOHN WILMOT, EARL OF ROCHESTER

63   *The Chimney-Sweeper's Complaint*   92
     MARY ALCOCK

64   *The Chimney-Sweeper*   94
     WILLIAM BLAKE

65   Song: *The Unconcerned*   95
     THOMAS FLATMAN

66   *Careless Content*   96
     JOHN BYROM

67   *Sonnet 16: On His Blindness*   99
     JOHN MILTON

68   *The Collar*   100
     GEORGE HERBERT

69   *Quickness*   102
     HENRY VAUGHAN

70   *Death the Leveller*   103
     JAMES SHIRLEY

71   *Sonnet: Death, Be Not Proud*   104
     JOHN DONNE

72   *Elegy Written in a Country Churchyard*   105
     THOMAS GRAY

73   *Kubla Khan*   110
     SAMUEL TAYLOR COLERIDGE

74   From *An Essay on Man*   112
     ALEXANDER POPE

PART 3

Poems from the Nineteenth and Twentieth Centuries (I)

75   *Caged Bird*   115
     MAYA ANGELOU

76   *Rising Five*   117
     NORMAN NICHOLSON

77   *Little Boy Crying*   119
     MERVYN MORRIS
78   *Carpet-weavers, Morocco*   120
     CAROL RUMENS
79   *Song to the Men of England*   121
     PERCY BYSSHE SHELLEY
80   From *Spectator Ab Extra*   123
     ARTHUR HUGH CLOUGH
81   *Monologue*   124
     HONE TUWHARE
82   *The Justice of the Peace*   126
     HILAIRE BELLOC
83   *Before the Sun*   127
     CHARLES MUNGOSHI
84   *Muliebrity*   129
     SUJATA BHATT
85   *She Dwelt Among the Untrodden Ways*   130
     WILLIAM WORDSWORTH
86   *Farmhand*   131
     JAMES K. BAXTER
87   *Plenty*   132
     ISOBEL DIXON
88   *Storyteller*   134
     LIZ LOCHHEAD
89   *Those Winter Sundays*   136
     ROBERT HAYDEN
90   *The Old Familiar Faces*   137
     CHARLES LAMB
91   *Mid-Term Break*   138
     SEAMUS HEANEY
92   *The Listeners*   139
     WALTER DE LA MARE
93   *Not Waving But Drowning*   141
     STEVIE SMITH
94   *The Three Fates*   142
     ROSEMARY DOBSON
95   *Elegy for Drowned Children*   143
     BRUCE DAWE
96   *The Voice*   144
     THOMAS HARDY
97   *Time*   145
     ALLEN CURNOW
98   *Dover Beach*   146
     MATTHEW ARNOLD
99   *Amends*   148
     ADRIENNE RICH

100   *Full Moon and Little Frieda*   149
      TED HUGHES
101   *Lament*   150
      GILLIAN CLARKE
102   *On The Grasshopper and The Cricket*   151
      JOHN KEATS
103   *The Flower-Fed Buffaloes*   152
      VACHEL LINDSAY
104   *Report To Wordsworth*   153
      BOEY KIM CHENG
105   *First Love*   154
      JOHN CLARE
106   *Marrysong*   155
      DENNIS SCOTT
107   *So, We'll Go No More A-Roving*   156
      GEORGE GORDON, LORD BYRON
108   *Sonnet 43*   157
      ELIZABETH BARRETT BROWNING
109   *Sonnet 29*   158
      EDNA ST VINCENT MILLAY

PART 4

Poems from the Nineteenth and Twentieth Centuries (II)

110   *A Different History*   161
      SUJATA BHATT
111   *Pied Beauty*   162
      GERARD MANLEY HOPKINS
112   *Continuum*   163
      ALLEN CURNOW
113   *Horses*   164
      EDWIN MUIR
114   *Hunting Snake*   166
      JUDITH WRIGHT
115   *Pike*   167
      TED HUGHES
116   *A Birthday*   169
      CHRISTINA ROSSETTI
117   *The Woodspurge*   170
      DANTE GABRIEL ROSSETTI
118   *The Cockroach*   171
      KEVIN HALLIGAN
119   *The City Planners*   172
      MARGARET ATWOOD

120   *The Planners*   174
      BOEY KIM CHENG
121   *Summer Farm*   175
      NORMAN MACCAIG
122   *Where I Come From*   176
      ELIZABETH BREWSTER
123   *Sonnet: Composed Upon Westminster Bridge*   177
      WILLIAM WORDSWORTH
124   *The Bay*   178
      JAMES K. BAXTER
125   *Where Lies the Land?*   179
      ARTHUR HUGH CLOUGH
126   *Morse*   180
      LES MURRAY
127   *The Man with Night Sweats*   181
      THOM GUNN
128   *Night Sweat*   182
      ROBERT LOWELL
129   *Rain*   183
      EDWARD THOMAS
130   *Any Soul to Any Body*   184
      COSMO MONKHOUSE
131   *The Spirit is too Blunt an Instrument*   186
      ANNE STEVENSON
132   From *Long Distance*   188
      TONY HARRISON
133   From *Modern Love*   189
      GEORGE MEREDITH
134   *Funeral Blues*   190
      W.H. AUDEN
135   *La Figlia Che Piange*   191
      T.S. ELIOT
136   From *Song of Myself*   192
      WALT WHITMAN
137   *He Never Expected Much*   194
      THOMAS HARDY
138   *The Telephone Call*   195
      FLEUR ADCOCK
139   *A Consumer's Report*   197
      PETER PORTER
140   *Request To A Year*   199
      JUDITH WRIGHT
141   *On Finding a Small Fly Crushed in a Book*   200
      CHARLES TENNYSON TURNER

142 *Ozymandias*   201
     PERCY BYSSHE SHELLEY
143 *Away, Melancholy*   202
     STEVIE SMITH

PART 5

Poems from the Nineteenth and Twentieth Centuries (III)

144 *Childhood*   207
     FRANCES CORNFORD
145 *Because I Could Not Stop For Death*   208
     EMILY DICKINSON
146 *One Art*   209
     ELIZABETH BISHOP
147 Song: *Tears, Idle Tears*   210
     ALFRED, LORD TENNYSON
148 *My Parents*   211
     STEPHEN SPENDER
149 *For Heidi With Blue Hair*   212
     FLEUR ADCOCK
150 *Praise Song For My Mother*   214
     GRACE NICHOLS
151 *Follower*   215
     SEAMUS HEANEY
152 *Elegy For My Father's Father*   216
     JAMES K. BAXTER
153 *The Trees Are Down*   218
     CHARLOTTE MEW
154 *The Trees*   220
     PHILIP LARKIN
155 *Country School*   221
     ALLEN CURNOW
156 *Cambodia*   222
     JAMES FENTON
157 *Attack*   223
     SIEGFRIED SASSOON
158 *Reservist*   224
     BOEY KIM CHENG
159 *You Cannot Do This*   226
     GWENDOLYN MACEWEN
160 *Anthem For Doomed Youth*   227
     WILFRED OWEN
161 *My Dreams Are Of A Field Afar*   228
     A.E. HOUSMAN

162 *Friend*   229
    HONE TUWHARE
163 *A Man I Am*   231
    STEVIE SMITH
164 *Here*   232
    R.S. THOMAS
165 *A Dream*   233
    WILLIAM ALLINGHAM
166 *Time's Fool*   235
    RUTH PITTER
167 *Cold In The Earth*   236
    EMILY BRONTË
168 *A Quoi Bon Dire*   238
    CHARLOTTE MEW
169 From *The Triumph of Time*   239
    A.C. SWINBURNE
170 *Meeting At Night*   241
    ROBERT BROWNING
171 *Because I Liked You Better*   242
    A.E. HOUSMAN
172 From *The Ballad of Reading Gaol*   243
    OSCAR WILDE

Index of First Lines   245

Introduction

Songs of Ourselves contains work by more than a hundred poets from all parts of the English speaking world. It goes beyond being a book for students following a course for an examination: it is simultaneously a wide-ranging collection of verse for the school library, a resource for teachers and students of literature and language, and a handy single volume compendium for the general reader. Drawn from four centuries, it covers a great variety of poetic forms, styles and subjects, as well as reflecting a great variety of cultures. All the choices provide something to enjoy for readers of all ages, including those for whom English is not their first language.

The anthology is arranged in five broad sections, each illustrating the varied and exciting ways that poets choose forms, structures and words to shape meaning. Within each section the poems have been loosely grouped by theme so that many different connections (not just thematic) may be made between them, increasing and enhancing the reader's enjoyment. The reader will find all human experience here: love in its many forms, relationships and human personalities; sickness, death and war; nature, animals and the environment; youth and age, the rich and the poor. Poems can offer innermost thoughts, feelings and insights into existence: memory and hope, joy, wonder, grief and reflection are all to be found within these pages.

Poetry anthologies tend to belong to one of two main types: anthologies that are standard and traditional, or anthologies that restrict themselves to the new and contemporary. *Songs of Ourselves* combines these two approaches but greatly extends the range of the pre-twentieth century poems usually included in such collections. This reflects something of the important work that has been done by scholars in recent years in retrieving many forgotten poets, challenging the traditional 'canon' of poetry. Many significant new voices have been emerging – for example, many women poets who had previously been written out of poetic history. The twentieth and early twenty-first century writing here spans the globe, drawing in poets who write in English from places as geographically far apart as New Zealand, the Caribbean, Canada, India, Singapore and South Africa, for example, but all part of a wider community of poets who write in English.

As you lift the lid on the poems in this anthology, we hope that you will enjoy the diversity of voices and continue to explore the world of poetry in English outside these pages.

A note on glosses to the poems

Poems whose content is too obscure, or with content that is too specialised have been deliberately avoided.

Short glosses have been provided where the meaning of words, phrases or names (such as mythological characters) might not be known.

It is assumed that readers will have access to and use a good dictionary, so only the most obviously obscure words have been glossed. The glosses provided could certainly be added to and reworded because that is the nature of poetry: one definition of poetry is that it is *untranslatable* writing.

Glosses should not be taken to indicate that glossed words have particular significance and the glosses do not attempt to 'explain the poem'. They have been deliberately kept to the minimum so that they do not distract from the experience of reading the poem. It is important that readers do not feel put off by not knowing every word of a poem on a first reading; students should be encouraged by the thought that the most sophisticated reader will often hesitate and wonder about a meaning, and the poet might want us to do just that.

It is always a good idea to return to a poem more than once: further readings invariably reveal new depths.

Separate support material for teachers using part(s) of this anthology for a course of study for University of Cambridge International Examinations (CIE) exams is available from CIE.

University of Cambridge International Examinations
1 Hills Road
Cambridge
CB1 2EU
United Kingdom

Telephone:	+44 1223 553554
Fax:	+44 1223 553558
E-mail:	International©ucles.org.uk
Website:	www.cie.org.uk

Acknowledgements

We would like to thank Stewart Eames, Noel Cassidy and Nick de Somogyi for their help in the making of this anthology.

Mary Wilmer and Tim Underhill
University of Cambridge International Examinations

Acknowledgements

"Where I Come From" by Elizabeth Brewster, reprinted by permission of Oberon Press, Ottawa, Canada.

"You Cannot Do This" by Gwendolyn MacEwen, permission for use granted by the author's family.

"A Consumer's Report" by Peter Porter, permission for use granted by the author.

"City Planners" by Margaret Atwood, reprinted by permission of Time Warner Book Group UK.

"Praise Song For My Mother" by Grace Nichols, reprinted by permission of Time Warner Book Group UK.

"The Spirit is Too Blunt an Instrument" by Anne Stevenson from *The Collected Poems: 1955–1995*, reprinted by permission of Bloodaxe Books, 2000.

"The Telephone Call" by Fleur Adcock from the *Poems 1960–2000*, reprinted by permission of Bloodaxe Books, 2000.

"Because I Could Not Stop For Death" by Emily Dickinson, reprinted by permission of the publishers and the Trustees of Amherst College from The Poems of Emily Dickinson, Thomas H. Johnson, ed., Cambridge, Mass.: The Belknap Press of Harvard University Press, Copyright © 1951, 1955, 1979 by the President and Fellows of Harvard College.

"Summer Farm" by Norman MacCraig from *Collected Poems*, published by Chatto & Windus. Used by permission of The Random House Group Limited.

"Childhood" by Frances Crofts, reprinted by permission of the Trustees of Mrs Frances Crofts Cornford Will Trust.

"Request To A Year" by Judith Wright from *A Human Pattern: Selected Poems*, reprinted by permission from ETT Imprint, Sidney 1999.

"Cambodia" by James Fenton, reprinted by permission from PFD, UK.

"Because I Like You Better" and "My Dreams Are Of A Field Afar" by A.E. Housman, reprinted by permission from The Society of Authors, the Literary Representative of the Estate of A.E. Housman.

"Continuum" and "Country School" by Allen Curnow from *Collected Poems*, reprinted by permission from Carcanet Press Limited.

"A Different History" and "Muliebrity" by Sujata Bhatt from Brunizem, reprinted by permission from Carcanet Press Limited.

"Morse" by Les Murray from *New Collected Poems*, reprinted by permission from Carcanet Press Limited.

"Time" by Allen Curnow from *Early Days Yet*, reprinted by permission from Carcanet Press Limited.

"Hunting Snake" by Judith Wright from *Collected Poems*, reprinted by permission from Carcanet Press Limited.

"Lament" by Gillian Clarke from *Collected Poems*, reprinted by permission from Carcanet Press Limited.

"Amends" from *Dark Fields of the Republic: Poems 1991–1995* by Adrienne Rich. Copyright©1995 by Adrienne Rich. Used by permission of W.W. Norton & Company Inc.

"Elegy For My Father's Father", Farmhand" and "The Bay" by James K. Baxter, reprinted by permission of J.C. Baxter, Oxford University Press, Australia and New Zealand, 1979.

"Those Winter Sundays". Copyright©1966 by Robert Hayden, from *Angle of Ascent: New and Selected Poems* by Robert Hayden. Used by permission of Liveright Publishing Corporation.

"One Art" from *The Complete Poems 1927–1979* by Elizabeth Bishop. Copyright © 1979, 1983 by Alice Helen Methfessel. Reprinted by permission of Farrar, Straus and Giroux, LLC.

"Caged Bird" by Maya Angelou, reprinted by permission of Time Warner Book Group UK.

"Plenty" by Isobel Dixon, permission for use granted by the author.

"Report To Wordsworth", "Reservist" and "The Planners" by Boey Kim Cheng from ISBN 981-232-793-2, Another Place @ 2004 Times Edition. Reprinted by permission of Marshall Cavendish International (Asia) Pte. Ltd.

"For Heidi with Blue Hair" by Fleur Adcock, reprinted by permission from Bloodaxe Books.

"Here" by R.S. Thomas from *Collected Poems,* reprinted by permission from J.M. Dent, division of Orion Publishing Group.

"Full Moon and Little Frieda" and "Pike" by Ted Hughes; "Horses" by Edwin Muir; "Funeral Blues" by W.H. Auden; "La Figlia Che Piange" by TS Eliot; "The Trees" by Philip Larkin; "The Man with Night Sweats" by Thom Gunn; "Night Sweat" by Robert Lowell; and "Mid-Term Break" by Seamus Heaney reprinted by permission from Faber and Faber.

"Carpet-weavers, Morocco" by Carol Rumens reprinted by permission from PFD, UK.

Part 1

*Poems from the Sixteenth
and Early Seventeenth Centuries*

1

Song: *Why So Pale and Wan, Fond Lover?*

SIR JOHN SUCKLING

Why so pale and wan, fond lover?
        Prithee, why so pale?
Will, when looking well can't move her,
        Looking ill prevail?
        Prithee, why so pale?

Why so dull and mute, young sinner?
        Prithee, why so mute?
Will, when speaking well can't win her,
        Saying nothing do't?
        Prithee, why so mute?

Quit, quit, for shame; this will not move,
        This cannot take her.
If of herself she will not love,
        Nothing can make her:
        The devil take her!

fond] foolish
prithee] please, may I ask

2

What Thing Is Love?

GEORGE PEELE

What thing is love? – for sure love is a thing.
It is a prick, it is a sting,
It is a pretty, pretty thing;
It is a fire, it is a coal,
Whose flame creeps in at every hole;
And, as my wit doth best devise,
Love's dwelling is in ladies' eyes,
From whence do glance love's piercing darts,
That make such holes into our hearts.

darts] the arrows shot by Cupid, the Roman god of love

3

Sonnet 11

LADY MARY WROTH

You endless torments that my rest oppress,
    How long will you delight in my sad pain?
    Will never Love your favour more express?
    Shall I still live, and ever feel disdain?
Alas, now stay, and let my grief obtain
    Some end; feed not my heart with sharp distress.
    Let me once see my cruel fortunes gain
    At least release, and long-felt woes redress.
Let not the blame of cruelty disgrace
    The honoured title of your godhead Love;
    Give not just cause for me to say a place
    Is found for rage alone on me to move.
O quickly end, and do not long debate
My needful aid, lest help do come too late.

blame] offence, sin

4

Song: *Sigh No More, Ladies*

WILLIAM SHAKESPEARE

Sigh no more, ladies, sigh no more,
　　Men were deceivers ever;
One foot in sea, and one on shore,
　　To one thing constant never.
　　　　Then sigh not so,
　　　　But let them go,
　　And be you blithe and bonny,
Converting all your sounds of woe
　　Into 'Hey nonny, nonny'.

Sing no more ditties, sing no more
　　Of dumps so dull and heavy;
The fraud of men was ever so,
　　Since summer first was leavy.
　　　　Then sigh not so,
　　　　But let them go
　　And be you blithe and bonny,
Converting all your sounds of woe
　　Into 'Hey nonny, nonny'.

blithe and bonny] merry and beautiful
'Hey nonny, nonny'] a cheerful chorus
ditties] songs
dumps] fits of depression
leavy] leafy, decked with foliage

5

Song: *Weep You No More, Sad Fountains*

ANONYMOUS

Weep you no more, sad fountains;
    What need you flow so fast?
Look how the snowy mountains
    Heaven's sun doth gently waste.
      But my sun's heavenly eyes
        View not your weeping,
        That now lies sleeping
      Softly, now softly lies
        Sleeping.

Sleep is a reconciling,
    A rest that peace begets:
Doth not the sun rise smiling
    When fair at even he sets?
      Rest you then, rest, sad eyes,
        Melt not in weeping,
        While she lies sleeping,
      Softly, now softly lies
        Sleeping.

what need you] what reason is there for you to
waste] erode
begets] engenders, produces
fair] finely
even] evening

6

When I Was Fair And Young

QUEEN ELIZABETH I

When I was fair and young, and favour graced me,
Of many was I sought their mistress for to be.
But I did scorn them all, and said to them therefore:
'Go, go, go, seek some otherwhere; importune me no more.'

How many weeping eyes I made to pine in woe;
How many sighing hearts I have not skill to show,
But I the prouder grew, and still this spake therefore:
'Go, go, go, seek some otherwhere; importune me no more.'

Then spake fair Venus' son, that brave victorious boy,
Saying: 'You dainty dame, for that you be so coy,
I will so pluck your plumes as you shall say no more:
"Go, go, go, seek some otherwhere; importune me no more".'

As soon as he had said, such change grew in my breast
That neither night nor day I could take any rest.
Wherefore I did repent that I had said before:
'Go, go, go, seek some otherwhere; importune me no more.'

favour] good looks
importune] solicit, proposition
spake] said, spoke
Venus] Roman goddess of love (mother of Cupid)
for that you be] since you are being
pluck your plumes] remove your finery
wherefore] for which

7

They Flee From Me, That Sometime Did Me Seek

SIR THOMAS WYATT

They flee from me, that sometime did me seek,
With naked foot stalking in my chamber.
I have seen them, gentle, tame, and meek,
That now are wild, and do not remember
That sometime they put themselves in danger
To take bread at my hand; and now they range,
Busily seeking with a continual change.

Thankèd be fortune it hath been otherwise,
Twenty times better; but once in special,
In thin array, after a pleasant guise,
When her loose gown from her shoulders did fall,
And she me caught in her arms long and small,
Therewith all sweetly did me kiss,
And softly said, 'Dear heart, how like you this?'

It was no dream, I lay broad waking,
But all is turned, thorough my gentleness,
Into a strange fashion of forsaking;
And I have leave to go, of her goodness,
And she also to use newfangleness.
But since that I so kindly am servèd,
I fain would know what she hath deservèd.

in special] in particular
guise] manner, way
small] slender
broad waking] wide awake
thorough] through, via
forsaking] abandonment
newfangleness] fashionable fickleness
kindly] appropriately
fain] gladly

8

Sonnet 61

MICHAEL DRAYTON

Since there's no help, come let us kiss and part;
Nay, I have done, you get no more of me,
And I am glad, yea, glad with all my heart
That thus so cleanly I myself can free;
Shake hands for ever, cancel all our vows,
And when we meet at any time again,
Be it not seen in either of our brows
That we one jot of former love retain.
Now at the last gasp of love's latest breath,
When, his pulse failing, Passion speechless lies,
When Faith is kneeling by his bed of death,
And Innocence is closing up his eyes;
Now if thou wouldst, when all have given him over,
From death to life thou mightst him yet recover.

there's no help] there's nothing for it
I have done] I have finished
yea] yes, indeed
latest] final
given him over] given him up for dead
yet] still

9

Song: *Go, Lovely Rose!*

EDMUND WALLER

Go, lovely rose!
Tell her that wastes her time and me
That now she knows,
When I resemble her to thee,
How sweet and fair she seems to be.

Tell her that's young,
And shuns to have her graces spied,
That hadst thou sprung
In deserts, where no men abide,
Thou must have uncommended died.

Small is the worth
Of beauty from the light retired;
Bid her come forth,
Suffer herself to be desired,
And not blush so to be admired.

Then die! that she
The common fate of all things rare
May read in thee;
How small a part of time they share
That are so wondrous sweet and fair!

resemble] compare
shuns] is reluctant
Suffer] allow

10

No Crooked Leg, No Bleared Eye

QUEEN ELIZABETH I

No crookèd leg, no blearèd eye,
No part deformèd out of kind,
Nor yet so ugly half can be
As is the inward suspicious mind.

out of kind] unnaturally

11

Sonnet 31

SIR PHILIP SIDNEY

With how sad steps, O Moon, thou climb'st the skies!
How silently, and with how wan a face!
What, may it be that even in heavenly place
That busy archer his sharp arrows tries?
Sure, if that long-with-love-acquainted eyes
Can judge of love, thou feel'st a lover's case,
I read it in thy looks; thy languished grace,
To me that feel the like, thy state descries.
Then, even of fellowship, O Moon, tell me,
Is constant love deemed there but want of wit?
Are beauties there as proud as here they be?
Do they above love to be loved, and yet
Those lovers scorn whom that love doth possess?
Do they call virtue there ungratefulness?

that busy archer] Cupid, the Roman love-god, who fired arrows of love
tries] tests
if that] if it is true that
case] situation
languished grace] graceful sadness
state] circumstance, situation
descries] discovers, betrays
of fellowship] in the name of solidarity
want of wit] stupidity

12

Written The Night Before His Execution

CHIDIOCK TICHBOURNE

My prime of youth is but a frost of cares;
    My feast of joy is but a dish of pain;
My crop of corn is but a field of tares;
    And all my good is but vain hope of gain;
My life is fled, and yet I saw no sun;
And now I live, and now my life is done.

The spring is past, and yet it hath not sprung;
    The fruit is dead, and yet the leaves be green;
My youth is gone, and yet I am but young;
    I saw the world, and yet I was not seen;
My thread is cut, and yet it is not spun;
And now I live, and now my life is done.

I sought my death, and found it in my womb,
    I looked for life, and saw it was a shade,
I trod the earth and knew it was my tomb,
    And now I die, and now I am but made:
The glass is full, and now my glass is run,
And now I live, and now my life is done.

tares] weeds
glass] hourglass (an early device to measure time, using sand running through a glass)

13

The Author's Epitaph, Made By Himself

SIR WALTER RALEIGH

Even such is time, which takes in trust
Our youth, our joys, and all we have,
And pays us but with age and dust,
Who in the dark and silent grave
When we have wandered all our ways
Shuts up the story of our days,
And from which earth, and grave, and dust,
The Lord shall raise me up, I trust.

14

A Litany In Time Of Plague

THOMAS NASHE

Adieu, farewell, earth's bliss;
This world uncertain is;
Fond are life's lustful joys;
Death proves them all but toys;
None from his darts can fly;
I am sick, I must die.
　　　　Lord, have mercy on us!

Rich men, trust not in wealth,
Gold cannot buy you health;
Physic himself must fade.
All things to end are made,
The plague full swift goes by;
I am sick, I must die.
　　　　Lord, have mercy on us!

Beauty is but a flower
Which wrinkles will devour;
Brightness falls from the air;
Queens have died young and fair;
Dust hath closed Helen's eye.
I am sick, I must die.
　　　　Lord, have mercy on us!

Litany] long prayer
Fond] foolish
Physic] medical skill
Helen] legendarily beautiful woman

Strength stoops unto the grave,
Worms feed on Hector brave;
Swords may not fight with fate,
Earth still holds ope her gate.
'Come, come!' the bells do cry.
I am sick, I must die.
                Lord, have mercy on us!

Wit with his wantonness
Tasteth death's bitterness;
Hell's executioner
Hath no ears for to hear
What vain art can reply.
I am sick, I must die.
                Lord, have mercy on us!

Haste, therefore, each degree,
To welcome destiny;
Heaven is our heritage,
Earth but a player's stage;
Mount we unto the sky.
I am sick, I must die.
                Lord, have mercy on us!

Hector] legendarily valiant warrior
ope] open
bells] church bells tolling a death
Wit] intelligence
wantonness] lewdness
art] skill
degree] level of society
heritage] inheritance
player] actor

15

Sonnet 19

LADY MARY WROTH

Come, darkest night, becoming sorrow best;
    Light, leave thy light, fit for a lightsome soul;
    Darkness doth truly suit with me oppressed,
    Whom absence' power doth from mirth control:
The very trees with hanging heads condole
    Sweet summer's parting, and of leaves distressed
    In dying colours make a grief-ful roll,
    So much, alas, to sorrow are they pressed.
Thus of dead leaves her farewell carpet's made:
    Their fall, their branches, all their mournings prove,
    With leafless, naked bodies, whose hues fade
    From hopeful green, to wither in their love:
If trees and leaves for absence mourners be,
No marvel that I grieve, who like want see.

lightsome] carefree
from mirth control] exercise power over happiness
condole] commiserate with
roll] catalogue
like want] a similar lack

16

From *Underwoods*

BEN JONSON

It is not growing like a tree
In bulk, doth make man better be,
Or standing long an oak, three hundred year,
To fall a log at last, dry, bald, and sere:
A lily of a day
Is fairer far in May
Although it fall and die that night;
It was the plant and flower of light.
In small proportions we just beauties see,
And in short measures life may perfect be.

just] proper

17

Song: *Fear No More The Heat O' Th' Sun*

WILLIAM SHAKESPEARE

Fear no more the heat o' th' sun
    Nor the furious winter's rages;
Thou thy worldly task hast done,
    Home art gone, and ta'en thy wages.
Golden lads and girls all must,
As chimney-sweepers, come to dust.

Fear no more the frown o' th' great;
    Thou art past the tyrant's stroke.
Care no more to clothe and eat;
    To thee the reed is as the oak.
The sceptre, learning, physic, must
All follow this and come to dust.

Fear no more the lighning flash,
    Nor th'all-dreaded thunder-stone;
Fear not slander, censure rash;
    Thou hast finished joy and moan.
All lovers young, all lovers must
Consign to thee and come to dust.

past the tyrant's stroke] beyond the reach of the tyrant's blow
ta'en] taken
The sceptre] symbol of power
physic] medical skill
thunder-stone] thunderbolt
censure rash] sharp criticism
Consign to] submit to the circumstance of

No exorciser harm thee!
Nor no witchcraft charm thee!
Ghost unlaid forbear thee!
Nothing ill come near thee!
Quiet consummation have,
And renownèd be thy grave!

Ghost unlaid forbear thee] may your soul rest untroubled
consummation] completion, fulfilment

18

A Song

THOMAS CAREW

Ask me no more where Jove bestows,
When June is past, the fading rose;
For in your beauty's orient deep
These flowers, as in their causes, sleep.

Ask me no more whither do stray
The golden atoms of the day;
For in pure love heaven did prepare
Those powders to enrich your hair.

Ask me no more whither doth haste
The nightingale when May is past;
For in your sweet-dividing throat
She winters, and keeps warm her note.

Ask me no more where those stars light,
That downwards fall in dead of night;
For in your eyes they sit, and there
Fixèd become, as in their sphere.

Ask me no more if east or west
The phoenix builds her spicy nest;
For unto you at last she flies,
And in your fragrant bosom dies.

Jove] the Roman god Jupiter
bestows] disposes of
orient] (1) (*noun*) sunrise; (2) (*adjective*) lustrous, brilliant
as in their causes] to the same extent as their origins
sweet-dividing] melodiously singing
winters] stays the winter
light] alight
sphere] what people believed to be the crystal sphere of the night-sky
phoenix] mythical bird that built its nest from spices, burnt itself, and was born from its own ashes

19

Walsingham

SIR WALTER RALEIGH

'As you came from the holy land
    Of Walsingham,
Met you not with my true love
    By the way as you came?'

'How shall I know your true love,
    That have met many one
As I went from the holy land,
    That have come, that have gone?'

'She is neither white nor brown,
    But as the heavens fair:
There is none hath a form so divine
    In the earth or the air.'

'Such an one I did meet, sir,
    Such an angelic face,
Who like a queen, like a nymph, did appear
    By her gait, by her grace.'

'She hath left me here alone,
    All alone, as unknown,
Who sometimes did me lead with herself
    And me loved as her own.'

nymph] legendary semi-divine maiden

'What's the cause that she leaves you alone
            And a new way doth take,
That sometime did you love as her own,
            And her joy did you make?'

'I have loved her all my youth,
            But now am old, as you see:
Love likes not the falling fruit.
            Nor the withered tree.'

'Know that love is a careless child,
            And forgets promise past:
He is blind, he is deaf when he list,
            And in faith never fast.

'His desire is a dureless content,
            And a trustless joy;
He is won with a world of despair,
            And is lost with a toy.

'Of womenkind such indeed is the love
            (Or the word *love* abused)
Under which many childish desires
            And conceits are excused.

'But true love is a durable fire,
            In the mind ever burning,
Never sick, never dead, never cold,
            From itself never turning.'

when he list] when it pleases him
fast] constant
dureless] transient
toy] unimportant thing

20

The Flowers That on The Banks and Walks Did Grow

AEMILIA LANYER

The flowers that on the banks and walks did grow
Crept in the ground, the grass did weep for woe;
The winds and waters seemed to chide together
Because you went away they knew not whither;
And those sweet brooks that ran so fair and clear,
With grief and trouble wrinkled did appear.
Those pretty birds that wonted were to sing,
Now neither sing, nor chirp, nor use their wing;
But with their tender feet on some bare spray,
Warble forth sorrow and their own dismay.
Fair Philomela leaves her mournful ditty,
Drowned in dead sleep, yet can procure no pity.
Each arbour, bank, each seat, each stately tree
Looks bare and desolate now for want of thee,
Turning green tresses into frosty grey,
While in cold grief they wither all away.
The sun grew weak, his beams no comfort gave,
While all green things did make the earth their grave.
Each brier, each bramble, when you went away,
Caught fast your clothes, thinking to make you stay.

chide together] quarrel with each other
wonted] accustomed
spray] twig, branch
Philomela] in Greek myth, Philomela was transformed into a nightingale, and sang of her cruel
    treatment by King Tereus
ditty] song
arbour] garden, flower-bed

Delightful Echo, wonted to reply
To our last words, did now for sorrow die.
The house cast off each garment that might grace it,
Putting on dust and cobwebs to deface it.
All desolation then there did appear,
When you were going, whom they held so dear.
This last farewell to Cookham here I give:
When I am dead thy name in this may live,
Wherein I have performed her noble hest,
Whose virtues lodge in my unworthy breast,
And ever shall, so long as life remains,
Tying my heart to her by those rich chains.

Echo] in Greek myth, Echo was a nymph who, in unrequited love, pined away till only her voice
remained
wonted] accustomed
Cookham] the home of the author's friend
hest] command, behest

21

Come Live with me, and be my Love

CHRISTOPHER MARLOWE

Come live with me, and be my love,
And we will all the pleasures prove
That valleys, groves, hills and fields,
Woods, or steepy mountains yields.

And we will sit upon the rocks,
Seeing the shepherds feed their flocks
By shallow rivers, to whose falls
Melodious birds sing madrigals.

And I will make thee beds of roses
And a thousand fragrant posies,
A cap of flowers, and a kirtle
Embroidered all with leaves of myrtle,

A gown made of our finest wool,
Which from our pretty lambs we pull,
Fair linèd slippers for the cold,
With buckles of the purest gold,

A belt of straw and ivy buds
With coral clasps and amber studs:
And if these pleasures may thee move,
Come live with me, and be my love.

The shepherd swains shall dance and sing
For thy delight each May morning:
'If these delights thy mind may move,
Then live with me, and be my love.'

falls] (1) waterfalls; (2) cadences
kirtle] dress
myrtle] an evergreen shrub
swains] country youths

22

Sonnet 54

EDMUND SPENSER

Of this world's theatre in which we stay,
My love like the spectator idly sits,
Beholding me, that all the pageants play,
Disguising diversly my troubled wits.
Sometimes I joy when glad occasion fits,
And mask in mirth like to a comedy:
Soon after, when my joy to sorrow flits,
I wail, and make my woes a tragedy.
Yet she, beholding me with constant eye,
Delights not in my mirth nor rues my smart:
But when I laugh she mocks, and when I cry
She laughs, and hardens evermore her heart.
What then can move her? If nor mirth nor moan,
She is no woman, but a senseless stone.

diversly] variously
smart] pain
nor . . . nor] neither . . . nor

23

What is Our Life?

SIR WALTER RALEIGH

What is our life? A play of passion;
Our mirth the music of division;
Our mothers' wombs the tiring-houses be,
Where we are dressed for this short comedy.
Heaven the judicious sharp spectator is,
That sits and marks still who doth act amiss;
Our graves that hide us from the searching sun
Are like drawn curtains when the play is done.
Thus march we, playing, to our latest rest,
Only we die in earnest – that's no jest.

music of division] music played between the acts of a play
tiring-houses] dressing rooms
judicious sharp] wisely critical
still] ever
latest] final

24

Sonnet 75

EDMUND SPENSER

One day I wrote her name upon the strand,
But came the waves, and washèd it away:
Again I wrote it with a second hand,
But came the tide, and made my pains his prey.
'Vain man,' said she, 'that dost in vain assay
A mortal thing so to immortalise;
For I myself shall like to this decay,
And eke my name be wipèd out likewise.'
'Not so,' quod I, 'let baser things devise
To die in dust, but you shall live by fame:
My verse your virtues rare shall eternise,
And in the heavens write your glorious name:
Where, whenas death shall all the world subdue,
Our love shall live, and later life renew.'

strand] beach
pains] troublesome labours
assay] attempt
eke] also
quod] said
devise] intend
eternise] render immortal
whenas] when

25

Song: *Spring, The Sweet Spring*

THOMAS NASHE

Spring, the sweet spring, is the year's pleasant king,
Then blooms each thing, then maids dance in a ring,
Cold doth not sting, the pretty birds do sing:
    Cuckoo, jug-jug, pu-wee, to-witta-woo!

The palm and may make country houses gay,
Lambs frisk and play, the shepherds pipe all day,
And we hear aye birds tune this merry lay:
    Cuckoo, jug-jug, pu-wee, to-witta-woo!

The fields breathe sweet, the daisies kiss our feet,
Young lovers meet, old wives a-sunning sit,
In every street these tunes our ears do greet:
    Cuckoo, jug-jug, pu-wee, to-witta-woo!
        Spring, the sweet spring!

Cuckoo, jug-jug, pu-wee, to-witta-woo!] the songs of the cuckoo, nightingale, lapwing, and owl
the palm and may] festival decorations
aye] ever
lay] song

26

Sonnet 18

WILLIAM SHAKESPEARE

Shall I compare thee to a summer's day?
Thou art more lovely and more temperate:
Rough winds do shake the darling buds of May,
And summer's lease hath all too short a date:
Sometime too hot the eye of heaven shines
And often is his gold complexion dimmed;
And every fair from fair sometime declines,
By chance, or nature's changing course, untrimmed.
But thy eternal summer shall not fade,
Nor lose possession of that fair thou ow'st;
Nor shall death brag thou wander'st in his shade,
When in eternal lines to time thou grow'st:
So long as men can breathe, or eyes can see,
So long lives this, and this gives life to thee.

temperate] moderate, evenly tempered
lease] terms of a tenancy agreement
the eye of heaven] the sun
every fair] all that is beautiful
untrimmed] (1) stripped of decoration; (2) thrown off balance
ow'st] possess, own
shade] darkness, shadow
this] this poem

27

Sonnet 73

WILLIAM SHAKESPEARE

That time of year thou mayst in me behold
When yellow leaves, or none, or few, do hang
Upon those boughs which shake against the cold,
Bare ruined choirs where late the sweet birds sang.
In me thou see'st the twilight of such day
As after sunset fadeth in the west:
Which by and by black night doth take away,
Death's second self that seals up all in rest.
In me thou see'st the glowing of such fire,
That on the ashes of his youth doth lie,
As the deathbed whereon it must expire,
Consumed with that which it was nourished by.
This thou perceivest, which makes thy love more strong,
To love that well which thou must leave ere long.

choirs] part of churches where hymns are sung
see'st] see
Consumed with] eaten up by

28

Song: *Blow, Blow, Thou Winter Wind*

WILLIAM SHAKESPEARE

Blow, blow, thou winter wind,
Thou art not so unkind
        As man's ingratitude;
Thy tooth is not so keen,
Because thou art not seen,
        Although thy breath be rude.
Heigh-ho, sing heigh-ho, unto the green holly;
Most friendship is feigning, most loving mere folly.
        Then heigh-ho, the holly,
        This life is most jolly!

Freeze, freeze, thou bitter sky,
That dost not bite so nigh
        As benefits forgot:
Though thou the waters warp,
Thy sting is not so sharp
        As friend remembered not.
Heigh-ho, sing heigh-ho, unto the green holly;
Most friendship is feigning, most loving mere folly.
        Then heigh-ho, the holly,
        This life is most jolly!

keen] sharp
rude] harsh
benefits forgot] neglected favours
warp] wrinkle (into ice)

29

The Procession of The Seasons

EDMUND SPENSER

So forth issued the seasons of the year.
　　First, lusty Spring, all dight in leaves of flowers
　　That freshly budded and new blooms did bear,
　　In which a thousand birds had built their bowers
　　That sweetly sung to call forth paramours,
　　And in his hand a javelin he did bear,
　　And on his head, as fit for warlike stours,
　　A gilt-engraven morion he did wear,
That, as some did him love, so others did him fear.

Then came the jolly Summer, being dight
　　In a thin silken cassock coloured green
　　That was unlinèd all, to be more light,
　　And on his head a garland well beseen
　　He wore, from which as he had chafèd been
　　The sweat did drop; and in his hand he bore
　　A bow and shafts, as he in forest green
　　Had hunted late the leopard or the boar
And now would bathe his limbs, with labour heated sore.

lusty] vigorous
dight] dressed
bowers] leafy glades, arbours
paramours] lovers
stours] encounters
morion] helmet
cassock] long coat
unlinèd] without a lining
well beseen] handsome of appearance
chafèd] heated
shafts] arrows
sore] painfully

Then came the Autumn all in yellow clad
    As though he joyèd in his plenteous store,
    Laden with fruits that made him laugh, full glad
    That he had banished hunger, which to-fore
    Had by the belly oft him pinchèd sore;
    Upon his head a wreath, that was enrolled
    With ears of corn of every sort, he bore,
    And in his hand a sickle he did hold
To reap the ripened fruits the which the earth had yold.

Lastly came Winter clothèd all in frieze,
    Chattering his teeth for cold that did him chill,
    Whilst on his hoary beard his breath did freeze;
    And the dull drops that from his purpled bill,
    As from a limbeck, did adown distil.
    In his right hand a tippèd staff he held
    With which his feeble steps he stayèd still,
    For he was faint with cold and weak with eld
That scarce his loosèd limbs he able was to wield.

to-fore] previously
pinchèd] tormented
corn] grain
yold] yielded
frieze] coarse woollen cloth
hoary] white with age
bill] nose
limbeck] apparatus for distilling
adown] downwards
stayèd] supported
still] always
eld] old age
loosèd] weakened

30

The Man of Life Upright

THOMAS CAMPION

The man of life upright,
　　Whose guiltless heart is free
From all dishonest deeds
　　Or thought of vanity;

The man whose silent days
　　In harmless joys are spent,
Whom hopes cannot delude
　　Nor sorrow discontent:

That man needs neither towers
　　Nor armour for defence,
Nor secret vaults to fly
　　From thunder's violence.

He only can behold
　　With unaffrighted eyes
The horrors of the deep
　　And terrors of the skies.

Thus scorning all the cares
　　That fate or fortune brings,
He makes the heaven his book,
　　His wisdom heavenly things;

Good thoughts his only friends,
　　His wealth a well-spent age,
The earth his sober inn
　　And quiet pilgrimage.

secret vaults] hiding-places
unaffrighted] unafraid
age] life

31

A Mind Content

ROBERT GREENE

Sweet are the thoughts that savour of content;
    The quiet mind is richer than a crown;
Sweet are the nights in careless slumber spent;
    The poor estate scorns fortune's angry frown:
Such sweet content, such minds, such sleep, such bliss,
Beggars enjoy, when princes oft do miss.

The homely house that harbours quiet rest;
    The cottage that affords no pride nor care;
The mean that 'grees with country music best;
    The sweet consort of mirth and music's fare;
Obscurèd life sets down a type of bliss:
A mind content both crown and kingdom is.

savour] taste
careless] untroubled
estate] level of society
mean] (1) lowly sort; (2) middle range in music
'grees with] agrees with, suits
consort] company (of musicians)
fare] provision, merriment
Obscurèd] anonymous
type] ideal sort

32

I Grieve, and Dare Not Show my Discontent

QUEEN ELIZABETH I

I grieve, and dare not show my discontent;
I love, and yet am forced to seem to hate;
I do, yet dare not say I ever meant,
I seem stark mute but inwardly do prate.
     I am and not, I freeze and yet am burned,
     Since from myself another self I turned.

My care is like my shadow in the sun:
Follows me flying, flies when I pursue it,
Stands and lies by me, doth what I have done;
His too familiar care doth make me rue it.
     No means I find to rid him from my breast,
     Till by the end of things it be suppressed.

Some gentler passion slide into my mind,
For I am soft and made of melting snow;
Or be more cruel, love, and so be kind.
Let me or float or sink, be high or low.
     Or let me live with some more sweet content,
     Or die and so forget what love ere meant.

stark] entirely
prate] chatter
turned] (1) fashioned; (2) became
care] (1) trouble, unhappiness; (2) carefulness, solicitude
rue] regret
or . . . or] either . . . or
ere] before

33

Song: *To Celia*

BEN JONSON

Drink to me only with thine eyes,
    And I will pledge with mine;
And leave a kiss but in the cup,
    And I'll not look for wine.

The thirst that from the soul doth rise
    Doth ask a drink divine,
But might I of Jove's nectar sup,
    I would not change for thine.

I sent thee late a rosy wreath,
    Not so much honouring thee
As giving it a hope that there
    It could not withered be.

But thou thereon didst only breathe
    And sent'st it back to me,
Since when it breathes and smells, I swear,
    Not of itself but thee.

ask] demand
Jove] Jupiter, the supreme god of Roman mythology
nectar] the drink of the gods
sup] drink

34

Golden Slumbers

THOMAS DEKKER

Golden slumbers kiss your eyes,
Smiles awake you when you rise.
Sleep, pretty wantons, do not cry,
And I will sing a lullaby:
Rock them, rock them, lullaby.

Care is heavy, therefore sleep you;
You are care, and care must keep you.
Sleep, pretty wantons, do not cry,
And I will sing a lullaby:
Rock them, rock them, lullaby.

wantons] naughty children
Care] (1) worldly preoccupation, sorrow; (2) the object of cherishing; (3) attentive solicitude
sleep you] go to sleep

35

Song: *Full Fathom Five*

WILLIAM SHAKESPEARE

Full fathom five thy father lies;
    Of his bones are coral made;
Those are pearls that were his eyes:
    Nothing of him that doth fade,
But doth suffer a sea-change
Into something rich and strange.
Sea nymphs hourly ring his knell:
    Ding-dong.
Hark! now I hear them – Ding-dong, bell.

Full fathom five] five fathoms' deep (1 fathom = 6 feet)
suffer] undergo
nymphs] in Greek myth, semi-divine maidens
knell] funeral bell

36

A Farewell To The Reader

ISABELLA WHITNEY

Good reader, now you tasted have
    And smelt of all my flowers,
The which to get some pain I took,
    And travailed many hours.
I must request you spoil them not,
    Nor do in pieces tear them;
But if thyself do loathe the scent,
    Give others leave to wear them.
I shall no whit be discontent,
    For nothing is so pure
But one or other will mislike,
    Thereof we may be sure.
If he for whom I gathered them
    Take pleasure in the same,
And that for my presumption
    My friends do not me blame;
And that the savour take effect
    In such as I do know,
And bring no harm to any else,
    In place where it shall go;
And that when I am distant far,
    It worn be for my sake;
That some may say, 'God speed her well
    That did this nosegay make.'

travailed] laboured
Give others leave to] allow others to
no whit] not in the least
mislike] fail to impress
savour] odour, bouquet
nosegay] bouquet of flowers

Part 2

Poems from the Seventeenth and Eighteenth Centuries

37

The Fly

WILLIAM BLAKE

Little Fly,
Thy summer's play
My thoughtless hand
Has brush'd away.

Am not I
A fly like thee?
Or art not thou
A man like me?

For I dance,
And drink, & sing,
Till some blind hand
Shall brush my wing.

If thought is life,
And strength & breath,
And the want
Of thought is death;

Then am I
A happy fly,
If I live
or if I die.

38

Shadows In The Water

THOMAS TRAHERNE

In unexperienced infancy
Many a sweet mistake doth lie:
Mistake though false, intending true,
A *seeming* somewhat more than *view*,
    That doth instruct the mind
    In things that lie behind,
And many secrets to us show
Which afterwards we come to know.

Thus did I by the water's brink
Another world beneath me think;
And while the lofty spacious skies,
Reversèd there, abused mine eyes,
    I fancied other feet
    Came mine to touch and meet;
As by some puddle I did play,
Another world within it lay.

Beneath the water people drowned,
Yet with another heaven crowned,
In spacious regions seemed to go,
Freely moving to and fro:
    In bright and open space
    I saw their very face;
Eyes, hands, and feet they had like mine;
Another sun did with them shine.

Shadows] images
unexperienced] inexperienced
intending] meaning
brink] edge
abused] misled
fancied] playfully imagined
crowned] surmounted, canopied

'Twas strange that people there should walk,
And yet I could not hear them talk;
That through a little watery chink,
Which one dry ox or horse might drink,
     We other worlds should see,
     Yet not admitted be;
And other confines there behold
Of light and darkness, heat and cold.

I called them oft, but called in vain;
No speeches we could entertain:
Yet did I there expect to find
Some other world, to please my mind.
     I plainly saw by these
     A new Antipodes,
Whom, though they were so plainly seen,
A film kept off that stood between.

By walking men's reversèd feet
I chanced another world to meet;
Though it did not to view exceed
A phantasm, 'tis a world indeed,
     Where skies beneath us shine,
     And earth by art divine
Another face presents below,
Where people's feet against ours go.

Within the regions of the air,
Compassed about with heavens fair,
Great tracts of land there may be found,
Enriched with fields and fertile ground;
     Where many numerous hosts,
     In those far distant coasts,
For other great and glorious ends,
Inhabit, my yet-unknown friends.

entertain] conduct
Antipodes] the supposed land-of-opposites situated on the underside of the globe
kept off] stood out
phantasm] shadowy vision
art] creative skill
Compassed about with] surrounded by
hosts] crowds of people
ends] purposes

O ye that stand upon the brink,
Whom I so near me, through the chink,
With wonder see: what faces there,
Whose feet, whose bodies, do ye wear?
    I, my companions, see
    In you another me.
They seemèd others, but are we;
Our second selves those shadows be!

Look how far off those lower skies
Extend themselves! Scarce with mine eyes
I can them reach. O ye, my friends,
What secret borders on those ends?
    Are lofty heavens hurled
    'Bout your inferior world?
Are ye the representatives
Of other people's distant lives?

Of all the playmates which I knew
That here I do the image view
In other selves, what can it mean?
But that below the purling stream
    Some unknown joys there be
    Laid up in store for me;
To which I shall, when that thin skin
Is broken, be admitted in.

second selves] alter egos
borders on] (*verb*) stands at the boundary of
'bout] about, around
inferior] lower
purling] twisting, curling
skin] surface

39

Ants (From *Dryades*)

WILLIAM DIAPER

Ants prudent bite the ends of hoarded wheat,
Lest growing seeds their future hopes defeat;
And when they conscious scent the gathering rains,
Draw down their windy eggs and pilfered grains;
With summer's toil and ready viands fill
The deepest caverns of their puny hill;
There lie secure, and hug the treasured goods,
And safe in laboured cells they mock the coming floods.

A thousand kinds unknown in forests breed,
And bite the leaves, and notch the growing weed;
Have each their several laws, and settled states,
And constant sympathies, and constant hates.
Their changing forms no artful verse describes,
Or how fierce war destroys the wandering tribes.
How prudent Nature feeds her various young,
Has been, if not untold, at least unsung.
To th'insect race the Muse her pain denies,
While prouder men the little ant despise.

windy] puffed up, growing
viands] supplies of food
kinds] sorts of life, species
notch] keep score of
the Muse] poetry
pain] careful labour

40

The Ant or Emmet

ISAAC WATTS

These emmets, how little they are in our eyes!
We tread them to dust, and a troop of them dies
    Without our regard or concern:
Yet, as wise as we are, if we went to their school,
There's many a sluggard, and many a fool,
    Some lessons of wisdom might learn.

They don't wear their time out in sleeping or play,
But gather up corn in a sunshiny day,
    And for winter they lay up their stores:
They manage their work in such regular forms,
One would think they foresaw all the frosts and the storms,
    And so brought their food within doors.

But I have less sense than a poor creeping ant
If I take not due care for the things I shall want,
    Nor provide against dangers in time:
When death or old age shall stare in my face,
What a wretch shall I be in the end of my days,
    If I rifle away all their prime?

Now, now, while my strength and my youth are in bloom,
Let me think what will serve me when sickness shall come,
    And pray that my sins be forgiven:
Let me read in good books, and believe and obey,
That when death turns me out of this cottage of clay,
    I may dwell in a palace in heaven.

emmet] ant
rifle away] ransack, squander
cottage of clay] i.e. the human body

41

The Grasshopper

ABRAHAM COWLEY

Happy insect, what can be
In happiness compared to thee?
Fed with nourishment divine,
The dewy morning's gentle wine!
Nature waits upon thee still,
And thy verdant cup does fill;
'Tis filled wherever thou dost tread,
Nature self's thy Ganymede.
Thou dost drink and dance and sing,
Happier than the happiest king!
All the fields which thou dost see,
All the plants, belong to thee;
All that summer hours produce,
Fertile made with early juice.
Man for thee does sow and plough;
Farmer he, and landlord thou!
Thou dost innocently joy,
Nor does thy luxury destroy;
The shepherd gladly heareth thee,
More harmonious than he.

still] always, ever
verdant] green
Ganymede] the cup-bearer to Jove, the supreme god of Greek myth
Farmer he, and landlord thou!] man merely labours on the land you own!
joy] revel

Thee country hinds with gladness hear,
Prophet of the ripened year!
Thee Phoebus loves, and does inspire;
Phoebus is himself thy sire.
To thee of all things upon earth,
Life is no longer than thy mirth.
Happy insect, happy thou,
Dost neither age nor winter know.
But when thou'st drunk and danced and sung
Thy fill the flowery leaves among
(Voluptuous and wise withal,
Epicurean animal!),
Sated with thy summer feast,
Thou retirest to endless rest.

hinds] female deer
Phoebus] the Greek sun-god
sire] father
Voluptuous] addicted to sensual pleasures
withal] moreover
Epicurean] devoted to pleasure

42

To The Virgins, To Make Much of Time

ROBERT HERRICK

Gather ye rosebuds while ye may,
 Old time is still a-flying;
And this same flower that smiles today
 Tomorrow will be dying.

The glorious lamp of heaven, the sun,
 The higher he's a-getting,
The sooner will his race be run,
 And nearer he's to setting.

That age is best which is the first,
 When youth and blood are warmer;
But being spent, the worse and worst
 Times still succeed the former.

Then be not coy, but use your time;
 And while ye may, go marry:
For, having lost but once your prime,
 You may for ever tarry.

tarry] linger, remain

43

The Call

JOHN HALL

Romira, stay,
And run not thus like a young roe away;
No enemy
Pursues thee, foolish girl, 'tis only I:
I'll keep off harms,
If thou'll be pleased to garrison mine arms.
What, dost thou fear
I'll turn a traitor? May these roses here
To paleness shred,
And lilies stand disguisèd in new red,
If that I lay
A snare wherein thou wouldst not gladly stay.
See, see, the sun
Does slowly to his azure lodging run;
Come, sit but here,
And presently he'll quit our hemisphere:
So, still among
Lovers, time is too short or else too long;
Here will we spin
Legends for them that have love-martyrs been;
Here on this plain
We'll talk Narcissus to a flower again.

roe] female deer
garrison] inhabit (as soldiers of their barracks)
shred] dissolve into pieces
azure] sky-blue
still] always, ever
Narcissus] in Greek myth, a beautiful youth who, thinking it a nymph, fell in love with his own
    reflection in a pool, jumped in, was drowned, and was turned into a flower

Come here, and and choose
On which of these proud plats thou would repose;
Here mayst thou shame
The rusty violets, with the crimson flame
Of either cheek,
And primroses, white as thy fingers, seek;
Nay, thou mayst prove
That man's most noble passion is to love.

proud plats] splendid patches of grass

44

Love

HENRY BAKER

Love's an headstrong wild desire
To possess what we admire:
Hurrying on without reflecting,
All that's just or wise neglecting.
Pain, or pleasure, it is neither,
But excess of both together;
Now, addressing, cringing, whining,
Vowing, fretting, weeping, pining,
Murmuring, languishing, and sighing,
Mad, despairing, raving, dying:
Now caressing, laughing, toying,
Fondling, kissing, and enjoying.
Always in extremes abiding,
Without measure, fond or chiding:
Either furious with possessing,
Or despairing of the blessing:
Now transported, now tormented,
Still uneasy, ne'er contented.
None can tell its rise, or progress,
Or its ingress, or its egress,
Whether by a look produced,
Or by sympathy infused.

measure] moderation
fond] foolishly doting
transported] sent into raptures
Still] always, ever
ingress . . . egress] entrance . . . exit

Fancy does so well maintain it,
Weaker reason can't restrain it,
But is forced to fly before it,
Or else worship and adore it.

Fancy] imagination
maintain] sustain the notion of
fly before] flee at the sight of

45

Song: *Love Armed*

APHRA BEHN

Love in fantastic triumph sat,
Whilst bleeding hearts around him flowed,
For whom fresh pains he did create,
And strange tyrannic power he showed:
From thy bright eyes he took his fire,
Which round about in sport he hurled;
But 'twas from mine he took desire,
Enough to undo the amorous world.

From me he took his sighs and tears,
From thee his pride and cruelty;
From me his languishments and fears,
And every killing dart from thee.
Thus thou and I the god have armed,
And set him up a deity;
But my poor heart alone is harmed,
Whilst thine the victor is, and free.

fantastic] (1) extravagant; (2) imagined
undo] destroy, utterly ruin
languishments] fits of misery

46

Song: *I Feed A Flame Within*

JOHN DRYDEN

I feed a flame within which so torments me
That it both pains my heart and yet contents me:
'Tis such a pleasing smart, and I so love it,
That I had rather die than once remove it.

Yet he for whom I grieve shall never know it,
My tongue does not betray, nor my eyes show it:
Not a sigh nor a tear my pain discloses,
But they fall silently like dew on roses.

Thus to prevent my love from being cruel,
My heart's the sacrifice as 'tis the fuel:
And while I suffer this to give him quiet,
My faith rewards my love, though he deny it.

On his eyes will I gaze, and there delight me;
While I conceal my love, no frown can fright me:
To be more happy I dare not aspire;
Nor can I fall more low, mounting no higher.

smart] pain

47

The Mower To The Glow-Worms

ANDREW MARVELL

Ye living lamps, by whose dear light
The nightingale does sit so late
And, studying all the summer night,
Her matchless songs does meditate;

Ye country comets, that portend
No war, nor prince's funeral,
Shining unto no higher end
Than to presage the grasses' fall;

Ye glow-worms, whose officious flame
To wandering mowers shows the way,
That in the night have lost their aim,
And after foolish fires do stray:

Your courteous lights in vain you waste,
Since *Juliana* here is come,
For she my mind hath so displaced
That I shall never find my home.

matchless] incomparable
meditate] rehearse
end] purpose
officious] dutiful
foolish fires] the *ignis fatuus* or 'will o' the wisp' (the flaming phosphorescence that appears over
    marshy ground); hence a delusive object

48

Her Window

RICHARD LEIGH

     Here first the day does break,
And for access does seek,
Repairing for supplies
To her new-opened eyes;
Then, with a gentle light
Gilding the shades of night,
Their curtains drawn, does come
To draw those of her room:
Both open, a small ray
Does spread abroad the day,
Which peeps into each nest,
Where neighbouring birds do rest,
Who, spread upon their young,
Begin their morning-song,
And from their little home
Nearer her window come;
While from low boughs they hop,
And perch upon the top;
And so from bough to bough,
Still singing as they go,
In praise of light and her
Whom they to light prefer,
By whose protection blest,
So quietly they nest
Secure, as in the wood,
In such a neighbourhood;

Repairing] returning with reinforcements
curtains] (1) eyelids; (2) drapes
spread abroad] widely distribute
spread upon] sitting over

While undisturbed they sit,
Fearing no hawk nor net,
And here the first news sing
Of the approaching spring –
The spring which ever here
Does first of all appear,
Its fair course still begun
        By her, and by the sun.

49

To One That Asked me Why I Loved J.G.

'EPHELIA'

Why do I love? Go, ask the glorious sun
Why every day it round the world doth run;
Ask Thames and Tiber why they ebb and flow;
Ask damask roses why in June they blow;
Ask ice and hail the reason why they're cold;
Decaying beauties, why they will grow old:
They'll tell thee fate, that everything doth move,
Enforces them to this, and me to love.
There is no reason for our love or hate:
'Tis irresistible as death or fate.
'Tis not his face: I've sense enough to see
That is not good, though doted on by me.
Nor is't his tongue that has this conquest won,
For that at least is equalled by my own.
His carriage can to none obliging be –
'Tis rude, affected, full of vanity,
Strangely ill-natured, peevish and unkind,
Unconstant, false, to jealousy inclined.
His temper could not have so great a power:
'Tis mutable, and changes every hour.
Those vigorous years that women so adore
Are past in him: he's twice my age and more.

Thames and Tiber] the rivers of London and Rome
damask] light-pink
blow] come into bloom
move] motivate
carriage] bearing, demeanour
rude] brash, uncivilised
unkind] unnatural

And yet I love this false, this worthless, man
With all the passion that a woman can
Dote on his imperfections: though I spy
Nothing to love, I love, and know not why.
Sure 'tis decreed in the dark book of fate
That I should love, and he should be ingrate.

ingrate] ungrateful

50

As Loving Hind That, Hartless, Wants Her Deer

ANNE BRADSTREET

As loving hind that, hartless, wants her deer
Scuds through the woods and fern with hearkening ear,
Perplexed, in every bush and nook doth pry,
Her dearest deer might answer ear or eye;
So doth my anxious soul, which now doth miss
A dearer dear, far dearer heart, than this,
Still wait with doubts, and hopes, and failing eye,
His voice to hear or person to descry.
Or as the pensive dove doth all alone
On withered bough most uncouthly bemoan
The absence of her love and loving mate,
Whose loss hath made her so unfortunate,
Even thus do I, with many a deep sad groan,
Bewail my turtle true, who now is gone:
His presence and his safe return still woos
With thousand doleful sighs and mournful coos.
Or as the loving mullet, that true fish,
Her fellow lost, nor joy nor life do wish,
But launches on that shore, there for to die,
Where she her captive husband doth espy;
Mine being gone, I lead a joyless life,

hind] female deer
hartless] i.e. without a hart, or male deer
hearkening] listening
wants] lacks
scuds] glides
descry] catch sight of
uncouthly] artlessly
turtle] turtle-dove
woos] attempts to achieve
nor . . . nor] neither . . . nor
launches on] rushes onto
captive] i.e. caught

I have a loving peer, yet seem no wife:
But worst of all, to him can't steer my course,
I here, he there, alas, both kept by force.
Return, my dear, my joy, my only love,
Unto thy hind, thy mullet, and thy dove,
Who neither joys in pasture, house, nor streams;
The substance gone, O me, these are but dreams!
Together at one tree, O let us browse,
And like two turtles roost within one house,
And like the mullets in one river glide:
Let's still remain but one, till death divide.
    Thy loving love and dearest dear,
    At home, abroad, and everywhere.

peer] companion, mate
browse] graze, feed on leaves

51

A Married State

KATHERINE PHILIPS

A married state affords but little ease;
The best of husbands are so hard to please:
This in wives' careful faces you may spell,
Though they dissemble their misfortunes well.
A virgin state is crowned with much content,
It's always happy as it's innocent:
No blustering husbands to create your fears,
No pangs of childbirth to extort your tears,
No children's cries for to offend your ears,
Few worldly crosses to distract your prayers.
Thus are you freed from all the cares that do
Attend on matrimony, and a husband too.
Therefore, Madam, be advised by me:
Turn, turn apostate to love's levity.
Suppress wild nature if she dare rebel,
There's no such thing as leading apes in hell.

careful] full of care
spell] observe
extort] extract forcibly
crosses] troubles
apostate] religious traitor
leading apes in hell] the proverbial fate of spinsters

52

Ode on Solitude

ALEXANDER POPE

Happy the man whose wish and care
A few paternal acres bound,
Content to breathe his native air,
    In his own ground.

Whose herds with milk, whose fields with bread,
Whose flocks supply him with attire,
Whose trees in summer yield him shade,
    In winter fire.

Blessed! who can unconcernedly find
Hours, days, and years slide soft away,
In health of body, peace of mind,
    Quiet by day.

Sound sleep by night; study and ease
Together mixed; sweet recreation
And innocence, which most does please,
    With meditation.

Thus let me live, unseen, unknown;
Thus unlamented let me die;
Steal from the world, and not a stone
    Tell where I lie.

paternal acres] inherited land

53

From A Dialogue Between a Squeamish Cotting Mechanic and His Sluttish Wife, In a Kitchen

EDWARD WARD

Husband   Is the fish ready? You're a tedious while;
Take care the butter does not turn to oil.
Lay on more coals, and hang the pot down lower,
Or 'twill not boil with such a fire this hour.
Is that, my dear, the saucepan you design
To stew the shrimps and melt the butter in?
Nouns! withinside as nasty it appears
As if't had ne'er been scoured this fifty years.
Rare hussifs! How confounded black it looks!
God sends us meat; the devil sends us cooks.

Wife   Why, how now, cot! Must I be taught by you?
Sure, I without you know what I've to do.
Prithee go mind your shop, attend your trade,
And leave the kitchen to your wife and maid.
O'erlook your 'prentices, you cot, and see
They do their work, leave cookery to me.
Is't fit a man, you contradicting sot,

Cotting Mechanic] interfering tradesman
Sluttish] dirty, untidy
this hour] for the next hour
design] intend
Nouns!] an exclamation ('God's wounds!')
Rare] unusual, wonderful (sarcastic)
hussifs] housewives
cot] meddler, interferer
Prithee] please
O'erlook] supervise
'prentices] apprentices
fit] appropriate
sot] dolt, fool

Should mind the kettle or the porridge-pot,
And run his nose in every dirty hole,
To see what platter's clean, what dish is foul?
Be gone, you prating ninny, whilst you're well,
Or, faith, I'll pin the dish-clout to your tail.

Husband   I'll not be poisoned by a sluttish quean. –
Hussy, I say, go scour the saucepan clean.
What though your mistress is a careless beast,
I love to have my victuals cleanly dressed! –
I will direct and govern, since I find
You're both to so much nastiness inclined.
I'd have you know I neither fear or matter
Your threatened dish-clouts or your scalding water.

Wife   Stand by, you prating fool, you damned provoker,
Or, by my soul, I'll burn you with the poker.
Must I be thus abused, as if your maid,
And called a slut before a saucy jade?
Gad, speak another word and, by my troth,
I'll spoil the fish and scald you with the broth.
The kitchen fire, alas! don't burn to please ye;
The saucepan is, forsooth, too foul and greasy!

Husband   Hussy, what I direct, you ought to do;
I'm lord and master of this house and you.
Do you not know that wise and noble prince,
King 'Hasuerus, made a law long since
That every husband should the ruler be
Of his own wife, as well as family?
How dare you then control my lawful sway,
When Scripture tells you woman should obey?
Therefore, I say, I'll have my fish well dressed,
After such manner as shall please me best,
Or, hussy, by this ladle, if I ha'n't,
I'll make you show good reason why I shan't.

prating ninny] chattering fool
dish-clout] dish-cloth
quean . . . hussy . . . jade . . . trull] strumpet, low woman
matter] pay attention to, heed
Gad] by God
by my troth] by my faith
direct] instruct
King 'Hasuerus] Ahasuerus, the Biblical name for Xerxes I
control] object to
ha'n't] have not

Wife	Pray clean the saucepan, you forgetful trull,
	I must confess it looks a little dull. –
	You shall not say I love this jarring life,
	You shall have no complaints against your wife.
	But prithee, husband, leave us and be easy,
	Ne'er doubt but I will cook your fish to please ye.
Husband	Since you repent your failings, I'll be gone,
	But prithee let the fish be nicely done.
	I buy the best and, whether roast or boiled,
	You know I hate to have my victuals spoiled.
Wife	My dear, I'll take such care that you shall find
	It shall be rightly ordered to your mind.

      I'm glad he's gone. Pox take him for a cot!
What wife would humour such a snarling sot?
Here, Katherine, take my keys, slip gently by
The Fox, and fetch a dram for thee and I.
Lay down the saucepan. Pah! It's clean enough
For such an old, ill-natured, stingy cuff.
Prithee ne'er value what thy master says;
You should not mind his cross-grained, foolish ways;
But when *I* bid you, hussy, you must run.
Now his back's turned, the kitchen is our own.
Bless me! how easily can a woman blind
And cheat a husband, if he proves unkind.
He thinks, poor cuckold, that he bears the rule,
When heaven knows I do but gull the fool.

victuals] food
humour] tolerate
The Fox] i.e. the name of a tavern
cuff] (slang) old miser
cross-grained] abrasive
gull] deceive

54

On My Dreaming of my Wife

JONATHAN RICHARDSON

As waked from sleep, methought I heard the voice
Of one that mourned; I listened to the noise.
I looked, and quickly found it was my dear;
Dead as she was, I little thought her there.
I questioned her with tenderness, while she
Sighed only, but would else still silent be.
I waked indeed; the lovely mourner's gone,
She sighs no more, 'tis I that sigh alone.

Musing on her, I slept again, but where
I went I know not, but I found her there.
Her lovely eyes she kindly fixed on me;
'Let Miser not be nangry then,' said she,
A language love had taught, and love alone
Could teach; we prattled as we oft had done,
But she, I know not how, was quickly gone.

With her imaginary presence blessed,
My slumbers are emphatically rest;
I of my waking thoughts can little boast:
They always sadly tell me she is lost.
Much of our happiness we always owe
To error; better to believe than know!
Return, delusion sweet, and oft return!
I joy, mistaken; undeceived, I mourn;
But all my sighs and griefs are fully paid,
When I but see the shadow of her shade.

little thought her] hardly thought of (seeing) her
Miser . . . nangry] (baby talk) Mister . . . angry

55

William and Margaret

DAVID MALLET

'Twas at the silent, solemn hour,
    When night and morning meet;
In glided Margaret's grimly ghost,
    And stood at William's feet.

Her face was like an April morn,
    Clad in a wintry cloud:
And clay-cold was her lily hand
    That held her sable shroud.

So shall the fairest face appear,
    When youth and years are flown:
Such is the robe that kings must wear,
    When death has reft their crown.

Her bloom was like the springing flower,
    That sips the silver dew;
The rose was budded in her cheek,
    Just opening to the view.

But love had, like the canker-worm,
    Consumed her early prime:
The rose grew pale, and left her cheek;
    She died before her time.

grimly] grim-looking
lily] white (as a lily)
sable] black
reft] snatched
bloom] complexion
canker-worm] maggot

'Awake!' she cried, 'thy true love calls,
       Come from her midnight grave;
Now let thy pity hear the maid
       Thy love refused to save.

'This is the dumb and dreary hour,
       When injured ghosts complain;
When yawning graves give up their dead
       To haunt the faithless swain.

'Bethink thee, William, of thy fault,
       Thy pledge, and broken oath:
And give me back my maiden vow,
       And give me back my troth.

'Why did you promise love to me,
       And not that promise keep?
Why did you swear my eyes were bright,
       Yet leave those eyes to weep?

'How could you say my face was fair,
       And yet that face forsake?
How could you win my virgin heart,
       Yet leave that heart to break?

'Why did you say my lip was sweet,
       And made the scarlet pale?
And why did I, young witless maid,
       Believe the flattering tale?

'That face, alas! no more is fair;
       Those lips no longer red:
Dark are my eyes, now closed in death,
       And every charm is fled.

faithless swain] inconstant lover
Bethink thee] consider
troth] betrothal
charm] aspect of beauty

'The hungry worm my sister is;
    This winding-sheet I wear:
And cold and weary lasts our night,
    Till that last morn appear.

'But hark! – the cock has warned me hence;
    A long and late adieu!
Come, see, false man, how low she lies,
    Who died for love of you.'

The lark sung loud; the morning smiled,
    And raised her glistering head:
Pale William quaked in every limb,
    And raving left his bed.

He hied him to the fatal place
    Where Margaret's body lay:
And stretched him on the grass-green turf,
    That wrapped her breathless clay.

And thrice he called on Margaret's name,
    And thrice he wept full sore:
Then laid his cheek to her cold grave,
    And word spake never more.

winding-sheet] shroud
glistering] shining
hied him] hurried
clay] body

56

The Widow

ROBERT SOUTHEY

Cold was the night wind, drifting fast the snows fell,
Wide were the downs and shelterless and naked,
When a poor wanderer struggled on her journey
    Weary and way-sore.

Drear were the downs, more dreary her reflections;
Cold was the night wind, colder was her bosom!
She had no home, the world was all before her,
    She had no shelter.

Fast o'er the bleak heath rattling drove a chariot,
'Pity me!' feebly cried the poor night-wanderer.
'Pity me, strangers! lest with cold and hunger
    Here I should perish.

'Once I had friends, – but they have all forsook me!
Once I had parents, – they are now in heaven!
I had a home once – I had once a husband –
    Pity me, strangers!

'I had a home once – I had once a husband –
I am a widow poor and broken-hearted!'
Loud blew the wind, unheard was her complaining,
    On drove the chariot.

On the cold snows she laid her down to rest her;
She heard a horseman, 'Pity me!' she groaned out;
Loud blew the wind, unheard was her complaining,
    On went the horseman.

downs] open land
Drear] bleak

Worn out with anguish, toil and cold and hunger,
Down sunk the wanderer, sleep had seized her senses;
There did the traveller find her in the morning,
     God had released her.

57

The Rights of Woman

ANNA LAETITIA BARBAULD

Yes, injured Woman! rise, assert thy right!
Woman! too long degraded, scorned, oppressed;
O born to rule in partial Law's despite,
Resume thy native empire o'er the breast!

Go forth arrayed in panoply divine,
That angel pureness which admits no stain;
Go, bid proud Man his boasted rule resign
And kiss the golden sceptre of thy reign.

Go, gird thyself with grace, collect thy store
Of bright artillery glancing from afar;
Soft melting tones thy thundering cannon's roar,
Blushes and fears thy magazine of war.

Thy rights are empire: urge no meaner claim –
Felt, not defined, and if debated, lost;
Like sacred mysteries which, withheld from fame,
Shunning discussion, are revered the most.

Try all that wit and art suggest to bend
Of thy imperial foe the stubborn knee;
Make treacherous Man thy subject, not thy friend;
Thou mayst command, but never canst be free.

in partial Law's despite] despite the sway of biased laws
panoply] magnificent armour
admits] allows
magazine] arsenal

Awe the licentious and restrain the rude;
Soften the sullen, clear the cloudy brow:
Be more than princes' gifts thy favours sued –
She hazards all, who will the least allow.

But hope not, courted idol of mankind,
On this proud eminence secure to stay;
Subduing and subdued, thou soon shalt find
Thy coldness soften, and thy pride give way.

Then, then, abandon each ambitious thought;
Conquest or rule thy heart shall feebly move,
In Nature's school, by her soft maxims taught
That separate rights are lost in mutual love.

licentious] lascivious, lewd
rude] harsh, uncivil
sued] sought for
She hazards all, who will the least allow] 'nothing ventured, nothing gained'
eminence] elevated ground (hence lofty status)
maxims] moral sayings

58

Song: *To Lucasta, Going to The Wars*

RICHARD LOVELACE

Tell me not, sweet, I am unkind,
    That from the nunnery
Of thy chaste breast and quiet mind,
    To war and arms I fly.

True, a new mistress now I chase,
    The first foe in the field;
And with a stronger faith embrace
    A sword, a horse, a shield.

Yet this inconstancy is such
    As you too shall adore;
I could not love thee, dear, so much,
    Loved I not Honour more.

unkind] (1) cruel; (2) unnatural

59

Ode: I Hate That Drum's Discordant Sound

JOHN SCOTT

> I hate that drum's discordant sound,
> Parading round, and round, and round:
> To thoughtless youth it pleasure yields,
> And lures from cities and from fields,
> To sell their liberty for charms
> Of tawdry lace, and glittering arms;
> And, when Ambition's voice commands,
> To march and fight, and fall, in foreign lands.
>
> I hate that drum's discordant sound,
> Parading round, and round, and round:
> To me it talks of ravaged plains,
> And burning towns, and ruined swains,
> And mangled limbs, and dying groans,
> And widows' tears, and orphans' moans;
> And all that Misery's hand bestows
> To fill the catalogue of human woes.

that drum] i.e. that used to 'drum up' recruits to the army
yields] provides, furnishes
swains] youths

60

From *Blenheim*

JOHN PHILIPS

Now from each van
The brazen instruments of death discharge
Horrible flames, and turbid streaming clouds
Of smoke sulphureous; intermixed with these
Large globous irons fly, of dreadful hiss,
Singeing the air, and from long distance bring
Surprising slaughter; on each side they fly
By chains connexed, and with destructive sweep
Behead whole troops at once; the hairy scalps
Are whirled aloof, while numerous trunks bestrow
Th'ensanguined field; with latent mischief stored,
Showers of grenadoes rain, by sudden burst
Disploding murderous bowels: fragments of steel,
And stones, and glass, and nitrous grain adust.

Blenheim] the Battle of Blenheim (1704)
van] forefront of an army
brazen] brass
turbid] opaque
globous irons] cannonballs
connexed] joined together ('irons . . . by chains connexed' = chainshot)
bestrow] litter
ensanguined] bloodied
latent] held within
grenadoes] grenades
Disploding] explosively scattering
bowels] contents
nitrous grain] gunpowder
adust] burnt, scorched

A thousand ways at once the shivered orbs
Fly diverse, working torment and foul rout
With deadly bruise, and gashes furrowed deep.
Of pain impatient, the high-prancing steeds
Disdain the curb, and flinging to and fro,
Spurn their dismounted riders; they expire
Indignant, by unhostile wounds destroyed.
      Thus through each army death in various shapes
Prevailed; here mangled limbs, here brains and gore
Lie clotted; lifeless some: with anguish these
Gnashing, and loud laments invoking aid,
Unpitied and unheard; the louder din
Of guns, and trumpets' clang, and solemn sound
Of drums, o'ercame their groans.

shivered] shattered, fragmented
diverse] variously
rout] disorder
curb] bridle
unhostile] unintentionally aggressive (compare 'friendly fire')

61

The Hunting of The Hare

MARGARET CAVENDISH, DUCHESS OF NEWCASTLE

Betwixt two ridges of ploughed land lay Wat,
Pressing his body close to earth lay squat.
His nose upon his two forefeet close lies,
Glaring obliquely with his great grey eyes.
His head he always sets against the wind:
If turn his tail, his hairs blow up behind,
Which he too cold will grow; but he is wise,
And keeps his coat still down, so warm he lies.
Thus resting all the day, till sun doth set,
Then riseth up, his relief for to get,
Walking about until the sun doth rise;
Then back returns, down in his form he lies.
At last poor Wat was found, as he there lay,
By huntsmen with their dogs which came that way.
Seeing, gets up, and fast begins to run,
Hoping some ways the cruel dogs to shun.
But they by nature have so quick a scent
That by their nose they trace what way he went;
And with their deep, wide mouths set forth a cry
Which answered was by echoes in the sky.
Then Wat was struck with terror and with fear,
Thinks every shadow still the dogs they were;
And running out some distance from the noise
To hide himself, his thoughts he new employs.

Betwixt] between
Wat] a traditional name for the hare (as 'Tom' is for a cat)
grow] cause to become
still] ever
relief] food, sustenance
form] a hare's nest or lair
scent] sense of smell

Under a clod of earth in sandpit wide,
Poor Wat sat close, hoping himself to hide.
There long he had not sat but straight his ears
The winding horns and crying dogs he hears:
Starting with fear up leaps, then doth he run,
And with such speed, the ground scarce treads upon.
Into a great thick wood he straightway gets,
Where underneath a broken bough he sits;
At every leaf that with the wind did shake
Did bring such terror, made his heart to ache.
That place he left; to champian plains he went,
Winding about, for to deceive their scent,
And while they snuffling were, to find his track,
Poor Wat, being weary, his swift pace did slack.
On his two hinder legs for ease did sit:
His forefeet rubbed his face from dust and sweat.
Licking his feet, he wiped his ears so clean
That none could tell that Wat had hunted been.
But casting round about his fair great eyes,
The hounds in full career he near him spies;
To Wat it was so terrible a sight,
Fear gave him wings, and made his body light.
Though weary as before, by running long,
Yet now his breath he ever felt more strong.
Like those that dying are, think health returns,
When 'tis but a faint blast which life out burns –
For spirits seek to guard the heart about,
Striving with death; but death doth quench them out.
Thus they so fast came on, with such loud cries,
That he no hopes hath left, nor help espies.
With that the winds did pity poor Wat's case,
And with their breath the scent blew from the place.
Then every nose is busily employed,
And every nostril is set open wide;
And every head doth seek a several way
To find what grass or track the scent on lay.

close] secretly
straight] immediately, straight away
Winding] blowing
doth] does
champian] unenclosed
espies] catches sight of

Thus quick industry, that is not slack,
Is like to witchery: brings lost things back.
For though the wind had tied the scent up close,
A busy dog thrust in his snuffling nose,
And drew it out, with it did foremost run;
Then horns blew loud, for the rest to follow on.
The great slow hounds, their throats did set a bass,
The fleet swift hounds as tenors next in place;
The little beagles they a treble sing,
And through the air their voice a round did ring,
Which made a consort as they ran along:
If they but words could speak, might sing a song:
The horns kept time, the hunters shout for joy,
And valiant seem, poor Wat for to destroy.
Spurring their horses to a full career,
Swim rivers deep, leap ditches without fear;
Endanger life and limbs, so fast will ride,
Only to see how patiently Wat died.
For why, the dogs so near his heels did get
That they their sharp teeth in his breech did set.
Then tumbling down, did fall with weeping eyes,
Gives up the ghost, and thus poor Wat he dies.
Men hooping loud such acclamations make
As if the devil they did prisoner take,
When they do but a shiftless creature kill,
To hunt, there needs no valiant soldier's skill.
But man doth think that exercise and toil,
To keep their health, is best, which makes most spoil;
Thinking that food and nourishment so good,
And appetite, that feeds on flesh and blood.

witchery] witchcraft
bass . . . tenor . . . treble] low, medium and high musical voices
beagles] hunting dogs
round] a song, shared by two or more voices
consort] group of musicians; concert
career] gallop
For why] the reason being
breech] rump
hooping] crying, shouting, whooping
acclamations] cries of praise
shiftless] helpless
makes most spoil] creates the most damage

When they do lions, wolves, bears, tigers see
To kill poor sheep, straight say they cruel be;
But, for themselves, all creatures think too few
For luxury, wish God would make them new –
As if that God made creatures for man's meat,
And gave them life and sense for man to eat;
Or else for sport, or recreation's sake,
Destroy those lives that God saw good to make;
Making their stomachs graves, which full they fill
With murdered bodies that in sport they kill.
Yet man doth think himself so gentle mild,
When of all creatures he's most cruel wild;
And is so proud, thinks only he shall live,
That God a godlike nature did him give,
And that all creatures for his sake alone
Was made for him to tyrannise upon.

As if that] as if it were the case that

62

From *A Satyr Against Mankind*

JOHN WILMOT, EARL OF ROCHESTER

Be judge yourself, I'll bring it to the test
Which is the basest creature, man or beast?
Birds feed on birds, beasts on each other prey,
But savage man alone does man betray.
Pressed by necessity, they kill for food;
Man undoes man to do himself no good.
With teeth and claws by nature armed, they hunt
Nature's allowance to supply their want,
But man with smiles, embraces, friendship, praise,
Most humanly his fellow's life betrays,
With voluntary pains works his distress,
Not through necessity but wantonness.
For hunger or for love they bite and tear,
Whilst wretched man is still in arms for fear.
For fear he arms and is of arms afraid,
From fear to fear successively betrayed,
Base fear, the source whence his best actions came,
His boasted honour and his dear-bought fame,
The lust of power to which he's such a slave
And for the which alone he dares be brave,
To which his various projects are designed,
Which makes him generous, affable, and kind,
For which he takes such pains to be thought wise,
And screws his actions in a forced disguise,
Leads a most tedious life in misery
Under laborious, mean hypocrisy.

Satyr] (1) an old spelling of 'satire'; (2) a creature who is part-animal and part-man (who might be
    seen as a narrator speaking against mankind)
in arms] i.e. armed with weapons
dear-bought] obtained at great cost

Look to the bottom of this vast design,
Wherein man's wisdom, power, and glory join:
The good he acts, the ill he does endure,
'Tis all from fear, to make himself secure.
Merely for safety, after fame they thirst,
For all men would be cowards if they durst,
And honesty's against all common sense:
Men must be knaves, 'tis in their own defence.

durst] dared
knaves] rogues, scoundrels

63

The Chimney-Sweeper's Complaint

MARY ALCOCK

A chimney-sweeper's boy am I;
    Pity my wretched fate!
Ah, turn your eyes; 'twould draw a tear,
    Knew you my helpless state.

Far from my home, no parents I
    Am ever doomed to see;
My master, should I sue to him,
    He'd flog the skin from me.

Ah, dearest madam, dearest sir,
    Have pity on my youth;
Though black, and covered o'er with rags,
    I tell you naught but truth.

My feeble limbs, benumbed with cold,
    Totter beneath the sack,
Which ere the morning dawn appears
    Is loaded on my back.

My legs you see are burnt and bruised,
    My feet are galled by stones,
My flesh for lack of food is gone,
    I'm little else but bones.

chimney-sweeper's boy] *Note*: children were routinely employed to clean chimneys, since they
    were small enough to crawl up into them
doomed] destined
sue to] petition, seek help from
ere] before
galled] injured, hurt

Yet still my master makes me work,
    Nor spares me day or night;
His 'prentice boy he says I am,
    And he will have his right.

'Up to the highest top,' he cries,
    'There call out *chimney-sweep*!'
With panting heart and weeping eyes,
    Trembling I upwards creep.

But stop! no more – I see him come;
    Kind sir, remember me!
Oh, could I hide me under ground,
    How thankful should I be!

'prentice] apprentice

64

The Chimney-Sweeper

WILLIAM BLAKE

A little black thing among the snow,
Crying 'weep, 'weep, in notes of woe!
Where are thy father and mother, say?
'They are both gone up to the church to pray.

'Because I was happy upon the heath
And smiled among the winter's snow,
They clothed me in the clothes of death
And taught me to sing the notes of woe.

'And because I am happy and dance and sing,
They think they have done me no injury:
And are gone to praise God and his priest and king,
Who make up a heaven of our misery.'

65

Song: *The Unconcerned*

THOMAS FLATMAN

Now that the world is all in amaze,
    Drums and trumpets rending heavens,
        Wounds a-bleeding, mortals dying,
        Widows and orphans piteously crying;
Armies marching, towns in a blaze,
    Kingdoms and states at sixes and sevens:
        What should an honest fellow do,
        Whose courage and fortunes run equally low?
Let him live, say I, till his glass be run,
    As easily as he may;
        Let the wine and the sand of his glass flow together,
    For life's but a winter's day;
Alas! from sun to sun
        The time's very short, very dirty the weather,
    And we silently creep away.
Let him nothing do he could wish undone,
And keep himself safe from the noise of a gun.

amaze] amazement (*literally* lost in a maze)
rending] tearing, splitting
at sixes and sevens] in a state of confusion
glass] hourglass (an early device to measure time, using sand running through a glass)

66

Careless Content

JOHN BYROM

I am content, I do not care,
    Wag as it will the world for me;
When fuss and fret were all my fare,
    It got no ground, as I could see:
So when away my caring went,
I counted cost, and was content.

With more of thanks, and less of thought,
    I strive to make my matters meet;
To seek what ancient sages sought,
    Physic and food, in sour and sweet:
To take what passes in good part,
And keep the hiccups from the heart.

With good and gentle-humoured hearts,
    I choose to chat where'er I come,
Whate'er the subject be that starts;
    But if I get among the glum,
I hold my tongue to tell the troth,
And keep my breath to cool my broth.

Wag] carry on its way
fare] provision, food, means of living
got no ground] made no profit
meet] suitable, sufficient
sages] wise people
Physic] medicine
troth] promise, pledge of faith

For chance or change, of peace or pain,
    For Fortune's favour or her frown;
For lack or glut, for loss or gain,
    I never dodge, nor up nor down:
But swing what way the ship shall swim,
Or tack about with equal trim.

I suit not where I shall not speed,
    Nor trace the turn of every tide;
If simple sense will not succeed,
    I make no bustling, but abide:
For shining wealth, or scaring woe,
I force no friend, I fear no foe.

Of ups and downs, of ins and outs,
    Of 'they're in the wrong' and 'we're in the right',
I shun the rancours and the routs,
    And, wishing well to every wight,
Whatever turn the matter takes,
I deem it all but ducks and drakes.

With whom I feast I do not fawn,
    Nor, if the folks should flout me, faint;
If wonted welcome be withdrawn,
    I cook no kind of a complaint:
With none disposed to disagree,
But like them best, who best like me.

glut] superfluity
nor . . . nor] neither . . . nor
tack] navigate (a ship)
trim] balance (of a ship)
suit not] don't fit in
speed] succeed, thrive
bustling] fuss
abide] stay
wight] person
deem] consider
ducks and drakes] game of skimming stones
fawn] grovel to
flout] abuse, mock
wonted] usual, customary

Not that I rate myself the rule
      How all my betters should behave;
But fame shall find me no man's fool,
      Nor to a set of men a slave:
I love a friendship free and frank,
And hate to hang upon a hank.

Fond of a true and trusty tie,
      I never lose where'er I link,
Though if a business budges by,
      I talk thereon just as I think:
My word, my work, my heart, my hand,
Still on a side together stand.

If names or notions make a noise,
      Whatever hap the question hath,
The point impartially I poise,
      And read or write, but without wrath;
For, should I burn or break my brains,
Pray, who will pay me for my pains?

I love my neighbour as myself,
      Myself like him, too, by his leave;
Nor to his pleasure, power or pelf,
      Came I to crouch, as I conceive:
Dame Nature doubtless has designed
A man the monarch of his mind.

Now taste, and try this temper, sirs,
      Mood it and brood it in your breast;
Or if ye ween, for worldly stirs,
      That man does right to mar his rest,
Let me be deft and debonair,
I am content, I do not care.

hank] restraining hold
business] commotion
hap] event, chance
pelf] money, riches
by his leave] if he will allow me
crouch] kneel in servile flattery
Mood . . . brood] reflect upon . . . consider
ween] believe
stirs] commotion, fuss
deft] gentle, skilful
debonair] airy, blithe, carefree

67

Sonnet 16: On His Blindness

JOHN MILTON

When I consider how my light is spent,
    Ere half my days, in this dark world and wide,
    And that one talent which is death to hide,
    Lodged with me useless, though my soul more bent
To serve therewith my maker, and present
    My true account, lest he, returning, chide;
    'Doth God exact day-labour, light denied?'
    I fondly ask: but Patience, to prevent
That murmur, soon replies, 'God doth not need
    Either man's work or his own gifts; who best
    Bear his mild yoke, they serve him best; his state
Is kingly – thousands at his bidding speed
    And post o'er land and ocean without rest:
    They also serve who only stand and wait.'

spent] extinguished
Ere] before
talent] artistic disposition
exact day-labour] commission work by the day
prevent] forestall
murmur] grumble
post] hasten

68

The Collar

GEORGE HERBERT

I struck the board, and cried, 'No more,
I will abroad!
What? shall I ever sigh and pine?
My lines and life are free, free as the road,
Loose as the wind, as large as store.
Shall I be still in suit?
Have I no harvest but a thorn
To let me blood, and not restore
What I have lost with cordial fruit?
Sure there was wine
Before my sighs did dry it; there was corn
Before my tears did drown it.
Is the year only lost to me?
Have I no bays to crown it?
No flowers, no garlands gay? All blasted?
All wasted?
Not so, my heart: but there is fruit,
And thou hast hands.

Collar] (1) an emblem of disciplined restraint (like both a dog's collar and a vicar's 'dog-collar');
    (2) a pun on 'Choler' = anger
board] dining table or communion table (at both of which the speaker serves)
lines] (1) routes, courses; (2) lines of poetry
suit] service
cordial] restorative
Sure] certainly
only] wholly
bays] garland of laurels, symbolising poetic excellence
blasted] blighted, withered

Recover all thy sigh-blown age
On double pleasures: leave thy cold dispute
Of what is fit, and not. Forsake thy cage,
Thy rope of sands,
Which petty thoughts have made, and made to thee
Good cable, to enforce and draw
And be thy law,
While thou didst wink and wouldst not see.
Away; take heed,
I will abroad,
Call in thy death's head there: tie up thy fears.
He that forbears
To suit and serve his need
Deserves his load.'
But as I raved and grew more fierce and wild
At every word,
Me thoughts I heard one calling, 'Child!'
And I replied, 'My Lord.'

rope of sands] fragile connection
wink] close one's eyes, be inattentive
death's head] the skull as an object of meditation about mortality
Me thoughts] it seemed to me that

69

Quickness

HENRY VAUGHAN

False life! a foil and no more, when
    Wilt thou be gone?
Thou foul deception of all men
That would not have the true come on.

Thou art a moon-like toil; a blind
    Self-posing state;
A dark contest of waves and wind;
A mere tempestuous debate.

Life is a fixed, discerning light,
    A knowing joy;
No chance, or fit: but ever bright
And calm and full, yet doth not cloy.

'Tis such a blissful thing that still
    Doth vivify
And shine and smile, and hath the skill
To please without eternity.

Thou art a toilsome mole, or less,
    A moving mist;
But life is, what none can express,
A quickness, which my God hath kissed.

foil] (1) shiny reflective surface; (2) dull background that sets off a jewel's brightness
moon-like] i.e. changeable, inconstant
self-posing] self-destructive
fit] passing convulsion
cloy] over-satisfy, sicken
still] always
vivify] come into life, render vivid, brighten
toilsome] hard-working, labouring
quickness] fleeting spirit

70

Death the Leveller

JAMES SHIRLEY

The glories of our blood and state
    Are shadows, not substantial things;
There is no armour against fate;
    Death lays his icy hand on kings;
        Sceptre and crown
        Must tumble down,
And in the dust be equal made
With the poor crooked scythe and spade.

Some men with swords may reap the field,
    And plant fresh laurels where they kill,
But their strong nerves at last must yield;
    They tame but one another still;
        Early or late
        They stoop to fate,
And must give up the murmuring breath
When they, pale captives, creep to death.

The garlands wither on your brow;
    Then boast no more your mighty deeds;
Upon Death's purple altar now
    See where the victor-victim bleeds.
        Your heads must come
        To the cold tomb;
Only the actions of the just
Smell sweet, and blossom in their dust.

Sceptre and crown] symbols of royalty and power
scythe and spade] symbols of manual labour

71

Sonnet: Death, Be Not Proud

JOHN DONNE

Death, be not proud, though some have called thee
Mighty and dreadful, for thou art not so;
For those whom thou think'st thou dost overthrow
Die not, poor Death, nor yet canst thou kill me.
From rest and sleep, which but thy pictures be,
Much pleasure – then from thee much more must flow,
And soonest our best men with thee do go:
Rest of their bones, and souls' delivery.
Thou art slave to fate, chance, kings, and desperate men,
And dost with poison, war, and sickness dwell,
And poppy or charms can make us sleep as well,
And better than thy stroke. Why swell'st thou then?
One short sleep past, we wake eternally,
And death shall be no more; Death, thou shalt die.

pictures] resemblances, images
then] it follows that
soonest] most readily
poppy] narcotics
swell'st] puff up with pride
charms] spells

72

Elegy Written in a Country Churchyard

THOMAS GRAY

The curfew tolls the knell of parting day,
The lowing herd wind slowly o'er the lea,
The ploughman homeward plods his weary way,
And leaves the world to darkness and to me.

Now fades the glimmering landscape on the sight,
And all the air a solemn stillness holds,
Save where the beetle wheels his droning flight,
And drowsy tinklings lull the distant folds;

Save that from yonder ivy-mantled tower
The moping owl does to the moon complain
Of such as, wandering near her secret bower,
Molest her ancient solitary reign.

Beneath those rugged elms, that yew-tree's shade,
Where heaves the turf in many a mouldering heap,
Each in his narrow cell for ever laid,
The rude forefathers of the hamlet sleep.

The breezy call of incense-breathing morn,
The swallow twittering from the straw-built shed,
The cock's shrill clarion or the echoing horn,
No more shall rouse them from their lowly bed.

curfew] the evening bell
knell] the funeral bell
lea] meadow
Save] except
folds] enclosures for sheep
bower] arbour, leafy glade
hamlet] small village

For them no more the blazing hearth shall burn,
Or busy housewife ply her evening care:
No children run to lisp their sire's return,
Or climb his knees the envied kiss to share.

Oft did the harvest to their sickle yield,
Their furrow oft the stubborn glebe has broke;
How jocund did they drive their team afield!
How bowed the woods beneath their sturdy stroke!

Let not Ambition mock their useful toil,
Their homely joys and destiny obscure;
Nor Grandeur hear, with a disdainful smile,
The short and simple annals of the poor.

The boast of heraldry, the pomp of power,
And all that beauty, all that wealth, e'er gave,
Awaits alike the inevitable hour.
The paths of glory lead but to the grave.

Nor you, ye Proud, impute to these the fault,
If Memory o'er the tomb no trophies raise,
Where through the long-drawn aisle and fretted vault
The pealing anthem swells the note of praise.

Can storied urn or animated bust
Back to its mansion call the fleeting breath?
Can Honour's voice provoke the silent dust,
Or Flattery soothe the dull cold ear of Death?

sire] father
stubborn glebe] clotted earth
jocund] cheerfully
team] i.e. of livestock, used for ploughing
annals] chronicles, history
trophies] memorial sculptures
fretted] intricately built
storied] tiered, raised on plinths
animated bust] lifelike sculpture

Perhaps in this neglected spot is laid
Some heart once pregnant with celestial fire;
Hands that the rod of empire might have swayed,
Or waked to ecstasy the living lyre.

But Knowledge to their eyes her ample page,
Rich with the spoils of time, did ne'er unroll;
Chill Penury repressed their noble rage,
And froze the genial current of the soul.

Full many a gem of purest ray serene
The dark unfathomed caves of ocean bear:
Full many a flower is born to blush unseen
And waste its sweetness on the desert air.

Some village-Hampden that with dauntless breast
The little tyrant of his fields withstood;
Some mute inglorious Milton here may rest,
Some Cromwell guiltless of his country's blood.

Th'applause of listening senates to command,
The threats of pain and ruin to despise,
To scatter plenty o'er a smiling land,
And read their history in a nation's eyes,

Their lot forbade: nor circumscribed alone
Their growing virtues, but their crimes confined;
Forbade to wade through slaughter to a throne,
And shut the gates of mercy on mankind,

The struggling pangs of conscious truth to hide,
To quench the blushes of ingenuous shame,
Or heap the shrine of Luxury and Pride
With incense kindled at the Muse's flame.

pregnant with] full of, inspired by
rod] sceptre
waked] brought into life
desert] deserted
Hampden . . . Milton . . . .Cromwell] notable anti-Royalist figures in the English Civil War: the
    statesman John Hampden; the poet John Milton; and the Lord Protector Oliver Cromwell
dauntless] fearless
circumscribed . . . confined] denied, restricted
ingenuous] guiltless, innocent

Far from the madding crowd's ignoble strife
Their sober wishes never learned to stray;
Along the cool sequestered vale of life
They kept the noiseless tenor of their way.

Yet even these bones, from insult to protect,
Some frail memorial still erected nigh,
With uncouth rhymes and shapeless sculpture decked,
Implores the passing tribute of a sigh.

Their name, their years, spelt by th'unlettered muse,
The place of fame and elegy supply:
And many a holy text around she strews,
That teach the rustic moralist to die.

For who, to dumb Forgetfulness a prey,
This pleasing anxious being e'er resigned,
Left the warm precincts of the cheerful day,
Nor cast one longing lingering look behind?

On some fond breast the parting soul relies,
Some pious drops the closing eye requires;
Even from the tomb the voice of Nature cries,
Even in our ashes live their wonted fires.

For thee who, mindful of th'unhonoured dead,
Dost in these lines their artless tale relate;
If chance, by lonely Contemplation led,
Some kindred spirit shall inquire thy fate,

Haply some hoary-headed swain may say,
'Oft have we seen him at the peep of dawn
Brushing with hasty steps the dews away
To meet the sun upon the upland lawn.

sequestered vale] secluded valley
tenor] routine
unlettered] illiterate
wonted] accustomed
Haply] perhaps
hoary-headed] white-haired
swain] countryman

'There at the foot of yonder nodding beech
That wreathes its old fantastic roots so high,
His listless length at noontide would he stretch,
And pore upon the brook that babbles by.

'Hard by yon wood, now smiling as in scorn,
Muttering his wayward fancies he would rove,
Now drooping, woeful wan, like one forlorn,
Or crazed with care, or crossed in hopeless love.

'One morn I missed him on the customed hill,
Along the heath, and near his favourite tree;
Another came; nor yet beside the rill,
Nor up the lawn, nor at the wood was he;

'The next with dirges due in sad array
Slow through the church-way path we saw him borne.
Approach and read (for thou canst read) the lay,
Graved on the stone beneath yon agèd thorn.'

The Epitaph

Here rests his head upon the lap of earth
A youth to fortune and to fame unknown.
Fair Science frowned not on his humble birth,
And Melancholy marked him for her own.

Large was his bounty and his soul sincere,
Heaven did a recompense as largely send:
He gave to Misery all he had, a tear;
He gained from heaven ('twas all he wished) a friend.

No farther seek his merits to disclose,
Or draw his frailties from their dread abode
(There they alike in trembling hope repose),
The bosom of his Father and his God.

yon] yonder, that one (over there)
rill] stream, brook
dirges due] appropriate laments
lay] song
Science] learning, wisdom
bounty] generosity

73

Kubla Khan

SAMUEL TAYLOR COLERIDGE

In Xanadu did Kubla Khan
A stately pleasure-dome decree:
Where Alph, the sacred river, ran
Through caverns measureless to man
    Down to a sunless sea.
So twice five miles of fertile ground
With walls and towers were girdled round:
And there were gardens bright with sinuous rills
Where blossomed many an incense-bearing tree;
And here were forests ancient as the hills,
Enfolding sunny spots of greenery.

But oh! that deep romantic chasm which slanted
Down the green hill athwart a cedarn cover!
A savage place! as holy and enchanted
As e'er beneath a waning moon was haunted
By woman wailing for her demon-lover!
And from this chasm, with ceaseless turmoil seething,
As if this earth in fast thick pants were breathing,
A mighty fountain momently was forced:
Amid whose swift half-intermitted burst
Huge fragments vaulted like rebounding hail,
Or chaffy grain beneath the thresher's flail:
And mid these dancing rocks at once and ever
It flung up momently the sacred river.

rills] streams, brooks
athwart] across from side to side
cedarn cover] thicket of cedar-trees
chaffy] like corn husks

Five miles meandering with a mazy motion
Through wood and dale the sacred river ran,
Then reached the caverns measureless to man,
And sank in tumult to a lifeless ocean:
And 'mid this tumult Kubla heard from far
Ancestral voices prophesying war!

The shadow of the dome of pleasure
Floated midway on the waves;
Where was heard the mingled measure
From the fountain and the caves.
It was a miracle of rare device,
A sunny pleasure-dome with caves of ice!

A damsel with a dulcimer
In a vision once I saw:
It was an Abyssinian maid,
And on her dulcimer she played,
Singing of Mount Abora.
Could I revive within me
Her symphony and song,
To such a deep delight 'twould win me
That with music loud and long,
I would build that dome in air,
That sunny dome! those caves of ice!
And all who heard should see them there,
And all should cry, Beware! Beware!
His flashing eyes, his floating hair!
Weave a circle round him thrice,
And close your eyes with holy dread,
For he on honey-dew hath fed,
And drunk the milk of Paradise.

dulcimer] stringed instrument

74

From *An Essay on Man*

ALEXANDER POPE

Know then thyself, presume not God to scan;
The proper study of mankind is man.
Placed on this isthmus of a middle state,
A being darkly wise, and rudely great:
With too much knowledge for the sceptic side,
With too much weakness for the stoic's pride,
He hangs between; in doubt to act or rest,
In doubt to deem himself a god or beast,
In doubt his mind or body to prefer,
Born but to die, and reasoning but to err;
Alike in ignorance, his reason such,
Whether he thinks too little or too much:
Chaos of thought and passion, all confused;
Still by himself abused or disabused;
Created half to rise and half to fall,
Great lord of all things, yet a prey to all;
Sole judge of truth, in endless error hurled:
The glory, jest, and riddle of the world!

scan] measure, contemplate
isthmus] a strip of land connecting two land-masses over the sea
sceptic] doubtful of the validity of human knowledge
stoic] one who suppresses emotion at life's disappointments

Part 3

Poems from the Nineteenth and Twentieth Centuries (I)

75

Caged Bird

MAYA ANGELOU

A free bird leaps
on the back of the wind
and floats downstream
till the current ends
and dips his wing
in the orange sun's rays
and dares to claim the sky.

But a bird that stalks
down his narrow cage
can seldom see through
his bars of rage
his wings are clipped and
his feet are tied
so he opens his throat to sing.

The caged bird sings
with a fearful trill
of things unknown
but longed for still
and his tune is heard
on the distant hill
for the caged bird
sings of freedom.

The free bird thinks of another breeze
and the trade winds soft through the sighing trees
and the fat worms waiting on a dawn-bright lawn
and he names the sky his own.

But a caged bird stands on the grave of dreams
his shadow shouts on a nightmare scream

his wings are clipped and his feet are tied
so he opens his throat to sing.

The caged bird sings
with a fearful trill
of things unknown
but longed for still
and his tune is heard
on the distant hill
for the caged bird
sings of freedom.

76

Rising Five

NORMAN NICHOLSON

'I'm rising five', he said,
'Not four', and little coils of hair
Un-clicked themselves upon his head.
His spectacles, brimful of eyes to stare
At me and the meadow, reflected cones of light
Above his toffee-buckled cheeks. He'd been alive
Fifty-six months or perhaps a week more:
                                        not four,
But rising five.

Around him in the field the cells of spring
Bubbled and doubled; buds unbuttoned; shoot
And stem shook out the creases from their frills,
And every tree was swilled with green.
It was the season after blossoming,
Before the forming of the fruit:
                            not May,
But rising June.

            And in the sky
The dust dissected tangential light:
                            not day,
But rising night;
                not now,
But rising soon.

rising five] nearly five years old
toffee-buckled] i.e. distorted by chewing toffee
swilled] rinsed
tangential] issuing at an angle

The new buds push the old leaves from the bough.
We drop our youth behind us like a boy
Throwing away his toffee-wrappers. We never see the flower,
But only the fruit in the flower; never the fruit,
But only the rot in the fruit. We look for the marriage bed
In the baby's cradle, we look for the grave in the bed:
                                        not living,
But rising dead.

77

Little Boy Crying

MERVYN MORRIS

Your mouth contorting in brief spite and
Hurt, your laughter metamorphosed into howls,
Your frame so recently relaxed now tight
With three-year-old frustration, your bright eyes
Swimming tears, splashing your bare feet,
You stand there angling for a moment's hint
Of guilt or sorrow for the quick slap struck.

The ogre towers above you, that grim giant,
Empty of feeling, a colossal cruel,
Soon victim of the tale's conclusion, dead
At last. You hate him, you imagine
Chopping clean the tree he's scrambling down
Or plotting deeper pits to trap him in.

You cannot understand, not yet,
The hurt your easy tears can scald him with,
Nor guess the wavering hidden behind that mask.
This fierce man longs to lift you, curb your sadness
With piggy-back or bull-fight, anything,
But dare not ruin the lessons you should learn.

You must not make a plaything of the rain.

78

Carpet-weavers, Morocco

CAROL RUMENS

The children are at the loom of another world.
Their braids are oiled and black, their dresses bright.
Their assorted heights would make a melodious chime.

They watch their flickering knots like television.
As the garden of Islam grows, the bench will be raised.
Then they will lace the dark-rose veins of the tree-tops.

The carpet will travel in the merchant's truck.
It will be spread by the servants of the mosque.
Deep and soft, it will give when heaped with prayer.

The children are hard at work in the school of days.
From their fingers the colours of all-that-will-be fly
and freeze into the frame of all-that-was.

garden of Islam] i.e. the carpet's abstract pattern

79

Song to the Men of England

PERCY BYSSHE SHELLEY

I
Men of England, wherefore plough
For the lords who lay ye low?
Wherefore weave with toil and care
The rich robes your tyrants wear?

II
Wherefore feed, and clothe, and save,
From the cradle to the grave,
Those ungrateful drones who would
Drain your sweat – nay, drink your blood?

III
Wherefore, Bees of England, forge
Many a weapon, chain, and scourge,
That these stingless drones may spoil
The forced produce of your toil?

IV
Have ye leisure, comfort, calm,
Shelter, food, love's gentle balm?
Or what is it ye buy so dear
With your pain and with your fear?

V
The seed ye sow, another reaps;
The wealth ye find, another keeps;
The robes ye weave, another wears;
The arms ye forge, another bears.

wherefore] why
drones] idlers (*literally* non-working, male honey-bees)
heap] pile up, hoard (money)

VI

Sow seed, – but let no tyrant reap;
Find wealth, – let no impostor heap;
Weave robes, – let not the idle wear;
Forge arms, – in your defence to bear.

VII

Shrink to your cellars, holes, and cells;
In halls ye deck another dwells.
Why shake the chains ye wrought? Ye see
The steel ye tempered glance on ye.

VIII

With plough and spade, and hoe and loom,
Trace your grave, and build your tomb,
And weave your winding-sheet, till fair
England be your sepulchre.

deck] decorate
tempered] rendered hard (of metal)
glance] strike at an angle
winding-sheet] shroud

80

From *Spectator Ab Extra*

ARTHUR HUGH CLOUGH

As I sat at the Café I said to myself,
They may talk as they please about what they call pelf,
They may sneer as they like about eating and drinking,
But help it I cannot, I cannot help thinking
        How pleasant it is to have money, heigh-ho!
        How pleasant it is to have money.

I sit at my table *en grand seigneur*,
And when I have done, throw a crust to the poor;
Not only the pleasure itself of good living,
But also the pleasure of now and then giving:
        So pleasant it is to have money, heigh-ho!
        So pleasant it is to have money.

They may talk as they please about what they call pelf,
And how one ought never to think of one's self,
How pleasures of thought surpass eating and drinking, –
My pleasure of thought is the pleasure of thinking
        How pleasant it is to have money, heigh-ho!
        How pleasant it is to have money.

Spectator ab extra] (Latin) the watcher from outside
pelf] money
en grand seigneur] (French) in the manner of a gentleman

81

Monologue

HONE TUWHARE

I like working near a door. I like to have my work-bench
      close by, with a locker handy.

Here, the cold creeps in under the big doors, and in the
      summer hot dust swirls, clogging the hose. When the
      big doors open to admit a lorry-load of steel,
      conditions do not improve. Even so, I put up with it,
      and wouldn't care to shift to another bench, away from
      the big doors.

As one may imagine this is a noisy place with smoke
      rising, machines thumping and thrusting, people
      kneading, shaping, and putting things together.
      Because I am nearest to the big doors I am the farthest
      away from those who have to come down to shout
      instructions in my ear.

I am the first to greet strangers who drift in through the
      open doors looking for work. I give them as much
      information as they require, direct them to the offices,
      and acknowledge the casual recognition that one
      worker signs to another.

I can always tell the look on the faces of the successful
      ones as they hurry away. The look on the faces of the
      unlucky I know also, but cannot easily forget.

I have worked here for fifteen months.
      It's too good to last.
      Orders will fall off
      and there will be a reduction in staff.

More people than we can cope with
will be brought in from other lands:
people who are also looking
for something more real, more lasting,
more permanent maybe, than dying. . . .
I really ought to be looking for another job
before the axe falls.

These thoughts I push away, I think that I am lucky
        to have a position by the big doors which open out
        to a short alley leading to the main street; console
        myself that if the worst happened I at least would
        have no great distance to carry my gear and tool-box
        off the premises.

I always like working near a door. I always look for a
        work-bench hard by – in case an earthquake
        occurs and fire breaks out, you know?

82

The Justice of the Peace

HILAIRE BELLOC

Distinguish carefully between these two,
    This thing is yours, that other thing is mine.
You have a shirt, a brimless hat, a shoe
    And half a coat. I am the Lord benign
Of fifty hundred acres of fat land
To which I have a right. You understand?

I have a right because I have, because,
    Because I have – because I have right.
Now be quite calm and good, obey the laws,
    Remember your low station, do not fight
Against the good, because, you know, it pricks
Whenever the uncleanly demos kicks.

I do not envy you your hat, your shoe.
    Why should you envy me my small estate?
It's fearfully illogical in you
    To fight with economic force and fate.
Moreover, I have got the upper hand,
And mean to keep it. Do you understand?

Justice of the Peace] magistrate
demos] populace, common people

83

Before the Sun

CHARLES MUNGOSHI

Intense blue morning
promising early heat
and later in the afternoon,
heavy rain.

The bright chips
fly from the sharp axe
for some distance through the air,
arc,
and eternities later,
settle down in showers
on the dewy grass.

It is a big log:
but when you are fourteen
big logs
are what you want.

The wood gives off
a sweet nose-cleansing odour
which (unlike sawdust)
doesn't make one sneeze.

It sends up a thin spiral
of smoke which later straightens
and flutes out
to the distant sky: a signal
of some sort,
or a sacrificial prayer.

The wood hisses,
The sparks fly.

And when the sun
finally shows up
in the East like some
latecomer to a feast
I have got two cobs of maize
ready for it.

I tell the sun to come share
with me the roasted maize
and the sun just winks
like a grown-up.

So I go ahead, taking big
alternate bites:
one for the sun,
one for me.
This one for the sun,
this one for me:
till the cobs
are just two little skeletons
in the sun.

84

Muliebrity

SUJATA BHATT

I have thought so much about the girl
who gathered cow-dung in a wide, round basket
along the main road passing by our house
and the Radhavallabh temple in Maninagar.
I have thought so much about the way she
moved her hands and her waist
and the smell of cow-dung and road-dust and wet canna lilies,
the smell of monkey breath and freshly washed clothes
and the dust from crows' wings which smells different –
and again the smell of cow-dung as the girl scoops
it up, all these smells surrounding me separately
and simultaneously – I have thought so much
but have been unwilling to use her for a metaphor,
for a nice image – but most of all unwilling
to forget her or to explain to anyone the greatness
and the power glistening through her cheekbones
each time she found a particularly promising
mound of dung –

Muliebrity] womanhood; female characteristics
canna lilies] large, leafy plants with bright flowers

85

She Dwelt Among the Untrodden Ways

WILLIAM WORDSWORTH

She dwelt among the untrodden ways
  Beside the springs of Dove,
A Maid whom there were none to praise
  And very few to love:

A violet by a mossy stone
  Half hidden from the eye!
– Fair as a star, when only one
  Is shining in the sky.

She lived unknown, and few could know
  When Lucy ceased to be;
But she is in her grave, and, oh,
  The difference to me!

Dove] name of a river

86

Farmhand

JAMES K. BAXTER

You will see him light a cigarette
At the hall door careless, leaning his back
Against the wall, or telling some new joke
To a friend, or looking out into the secret night.

But always his eyes turn
To the dance floor and the girls drifting like flowers
Before the music that tears
Slowly in his mind an old wound open.

His red sunburnt face and hairy hands
Were not made for dancing or love-making
But rather the earth wave breaking
To the plough, and crops slow-growing as his mind.

He has no girl to run her fingers through
His sandy hair, and giggle at his side
When Sunday couples walk. Instead
He has his awkward hopes, his envious dreams to yarn to.

But ah in harvest watch him
Forking stooks, effortless and strong –
Or listening like a lover to the song
Clear, without fault, of a new tractor engine.

yarn] spin thread (or a story)
stooks] bundles of hay

87

Plenty

ISOBEL DIXON

When I was young and there were five of us,
all running riot to my mother's quiet despair,
our old enamel tub, age-stained and pocked
upon its griffin claws, was never full.

Such plenty was too dear in our expanse of drought
where dams leaked dry and windmills stalled.
Like Mommy's smile. Her lips stretched back
and anchored down, in anger at some fault –

of mine, I thought – not knowing then
it was a clasp to keep us all from chaos.
She saw it always, snapping locks and straps,
the spilling: sums and worries, shopping lists

for aspirin, porridge, petrol, bread.
Even the toilet paper counted,
and each month was weeks too long.
Her mouth a lid clamped hard on this.

We thought her mean. Skipped chores,
swiped biscuits – best of all
when she was out of earshot
stole another precious inch

griffin] a mythical creature: a lion with an eagle's head and wings
clasp] fastening clip

up to our chests, such lovely sin,
lolling luxuriant in secret warmth
disgorged from fat brass taps,
our old compliant co-conspirators.

Now bubbles lap my chin. I am a sybarite.
The shower's a hot cascade
and water's plentiful, to excess, almost, here.
I leave the heating on.

And miss my scattered sisters,
all those bathroom squabbles and, at last,
my mother's smile, loosed from the bonds
of lean, dry times and our long childhood.

sybarite] one devoted to luxury

88

Storyteller

LIZ LOCHHEAD

she sat down
at the scoured table
in the swept kitchen
beside the dresser with its cracked delft.
And every last crumb of daylight was salted away.

No one could say the stories were useless
for as the tongue clacked
five or forty fingers stitched
corn was grated from the husk
patchwork was pieced
or the darning done.

Never the one to slander her shiftless.
Daily sloven or spotless no matter whether
dishwater or tasty was her soup.
To tell the stories was her work.
It was like spinning,
gathering thin air to the singlest strongest
thread. Night in
she'd have us waiting, held
breath, for the ending we knew by heart.

And at first light
as the women stirred themselves to build the fire
as the peasant's feet felt for clogs

dresser] kitchen shelves displaying dishes
delft] old earthenware
salted away] scrupulously stored

as thin grey washed over flat fields
the stories dissolved in the whorl of the ear
but they
hung themselves upside down
in the sleeping heads of the children
till they flew again
in the storytellers night.

whorl] coiled form

89

Those Winter Sundays

ROBERT HAYDEN

Sundays too my father got up early
and put his clothes on in the blueblack cold,
then with cracked hands that ached
from labor in the weekday weather made
banked fires blaze. No one ever thanked him.

I'd wake and hear the cold splintering, breaking.
When the rooms were warm, he'd call,
and slowly I would rise and dress,
fearing the chronic angers of that house,

Speaking indifferently to him,
who had driven out the cold
and polished my good shoes as well.
What did I know, what did I know
of love's austere and lonely offices?

banked] heaped with dust to ensure a slow burn; smouldering
offices] practical duties

90

The Old Familiar Faces

CHARLES LAMB

I have had playmates, I have had companions,
In my days of childhood, in my joyful school-days;
    All, all are gone, the old familiar faces.

I have been laughing, I have been carousing,
Drinking late, sitting late, with my bosom cronies;
    All, all are gone, the old familiar faces.

I loved a love once, fairest among women:
Closed are her doors on me, I must not see her –
    All, all are gone, the old familiar faces.

I have a friend, a kinder friend has no man:
Like an ingrate, I left my friend abruptly;
    Left him, to muse on the old familiar faces.

Ghost-like I paced round the haunts of my childhood,
Earth seemed a desert I was bound to traverse,
    Seeking to find the old familiar faces.

Friend of my bosom, thou more than a brother,
Why wert not thou born in my father's dwelling?
    So might we talk of the old familiar faces.

How some they have died, and some they have left me,
And some are taken from me; all are departed;
    All, all are gone, the old familiar faces.

carousing] making merry
bosom cronies] close friends
ingrate] ungrateful person
wert] were

91

Mid-Term Break

SEAMUS HEANEY

I sat all morning in the college sick bay
Counting bells knelling classes to a close.
At two o'clock our neighbours drove me home.

In the porch I met my father crying –
He had always taken funerals in his stride –
And Big Jim Evans saying it was a hard blow.

The baby cooed and laughed and rocked the pram
When I came in, and I was embarrassed
By old men standing up to shake my hand

And tell me they were 'sorry for my trouble'.
Whispers informed strangers I was the eldest,
Away at school, as my mother held my hand

In hers and coughed out angry tearless sighs.
At ten o'clock the ambulance arrived
With the corpse, stanched and bandaged by the nurses.

Next morning I went up into the room. Snowdrops
And candles soothed the bedside; I saw him
For the first time in six weeks. Paler now,

Wearing a poppy bruise on his left temple,
He lay in the four foot box as in his cot.
No gaudy scars, the bumper knocked him clear.

A four foot box, a foot for every year.

knelling] tolling (as for a funeral)
cot] child's bed
bumper] protective bar on a car

92

The Listeners

WALTER DE LA MARE

'Is there anybody there?' said the Traveller,
    Knocking on the moonlit door;
And his horse in the silence champed the grasses
    Of the forest's ferny floor.
And a bird flew up out of the turret,
    Above the Traveller's head:
And he smote upon the door again a second time;
    'Is there anybody there?' he said.
But no one descended to the Traveller;
    No head from the leaf-fringed sill
Leaned over and looked into his grey eyes,
    Where he stood perplexed and still.
But only a host of phantom listeners
    That dwelt in the lone house then
Stood listening in the quiet of the moonlight
    To that voice from the world of men:
Stood thronging the faint moonbeams on the dark stair,
    That goes down to the empty hall,
Hearkening in an air stirred and shaken
    By the lonely Traveller's call.
And he felt in his heart their strangeness,
    Their stillness answering his cry,
While his horse moved, cropping the dark turf,
    'Neath the starred and leafy sky;
For he suddenly smote on the door, even
    Louder, and lifted his head: –
'Tell them I came, and no one answered,
    That I kept my word,' he said.

ferny] covered with ferns
champed] chewed
Hearkening] listening

Never the least stir made the listeners,
  Though every word he spake
Fell echoing through the shadowiness of the still house
  From the one man left awake:
Ay, they heard his foot upon the stirrup,
  And the sound of iron on stone,
And how silence surged softly backward,
  When the plunging hoofs were gone.

93

Not Waving But Drowning

STEVIE SMITH

Nobody heard him, the dead man,
But still he lay moaning:
I was much further out than you thought
And not waving but drowning.

Poor chap, he'd always loved larking
And now he's dead
It must have been too cold for him his heart gave way,
They said.

Oh, no no no, it was too cold always
(Still the dead one lay moaning)
I was much too far out all my life
And not waving but drowning.

larking] larking about, indulging in playful behaviour

94

The Three Fates

ROSEMARY DOBSON

At the instant of drowning he invoked the three sisters.
It was a mistake, an aberration, to cry out for
Life everlasting.

He came up like a cork and back to the river-bank,
Put on his clothes in reverse order,
Returned to the house.

He suffered the enormous agonies of passion
Writing poems from the end backwards,
Brushing away tears that had not yet fallen.

Loving her wildly as the day regressed towards morning
He watched her swinging in the garden, growing younger,
Bare-foot, straw-hatted.

And when she was gone and the house and the swing and daylight
There was an instant's pause before it began all over,
The reel unrolling towards the river.

The Three Fates] in Greek myth, the three sisters who drew, spun, and cut the threads of our birth,
    life, and death
reel] spindle of thread

95

Elegy for Drowned Children

BRUCE DAWE

What does he do with them all, the old king:
Having such a shining haul of boys in his sure net,
How does he keep them happy, lead them to forget
The world above, the aching air, birds, spring?

Tender and solicitous must be his care
For these whom he takes down into his kingdom one by one
– Why else would they be taken out of the sweet sun,
Drowning towards him, water plaiting their hair?

Unless he loved them deeply how could he withstand
The voices of parents calling, calling like birds by the water's edge,
By swimming-pool, sand-bar, river-bank, rocky ledge,
The little heaps of clothes, the futures carefully planned?

Yet even an old acquisitive king must feel
Remorse poisoning his joy, since he allows
Particular boys each evening to arouse
From leaden-lidded sleep, softly to steal

Away to the whispering shore, there to plunge in,
And fluid as porpoises swim upward, upward through the dividing
Waters until, soon, each back home is striding
Over thresholds of welcome dream with wet and moonlit skin.

sand-bar] sand bank

96

The Voice

THOMAS HARDY

Woman much missed, how you call to me, call to me,
Saying that now you are not as you were
When you had changed from the one who was all to me,
But as at first, when our day was fair.

Can it be you that I hear? Let me view you, then,
Standing as when I drew near to the town
Where you would wait for me: yes, as I knew you then,
Even to the original air-blue gown!

Or is it only the breeze, in its listlessness
Travelling across the wet mead to me here,
You being ever dissolved to wan wistlessness,
Heard no more again far or near?

    Thus I; faltering forward,
    Leaves around me falling,
Wind oozing thin through the thorn from norward,
    And the woman calling.

mead] field, meadow
wistlessness] inattentiveness
norward] northern parts

97

Time

ALLEN CURNOW

I am the nor'west air nosing among the pines
I am the water-race and the rust on railway lines
I am the mileage recorded on the yellow signs.

I am dust, I am distance, I am lupins back of the beach
I am the sums the sole-charge teachers teach
I am cows called to milking and the magpie's screech.

I am nine o'clock in the morning when the office is clean
I am the slap of the belting and the smell of the machine
I am the place in the park where the lovers were seen.

I am recurrent music the children hear
I am level noises in the remembering ear
I am the sawmill and the passionate second gear.

I, Time, am all these, yet these exist
Among my mountainous fabrics like a mist,
So do they the measurable world resist.

I, Time, call down, condense, confer
On the willing memory the shapes these were:
I, more than your conscious carrier,

Am island, am sea, am father, farm, and friend,
Though I am here all things my coming attend;
I am, you have heard it, the Beginning and the End.

lupins] type of garden flower

98

Dover Beach

MATTHEW ARNOLD

The sea is calm to-night.
The tide is full, the moon lies fair
Upon the straits; – on the French coast the light
Gleams and is gone; the cliffs of England stand,
Glimmering and vast, out in the tranquil bay.
Come to the window, sweet is the night-air!

Only, from the long line of spray
Where the sea meets the moon-blanched land,
Listen! you hear the grating roar
Of pebbles which the waves draw back, and fling,
At their return, up the high strand,
Begin, and cease, and then again begin,
With tremulous cadence slow, and bring
The eternal note of sadness in.

Sophocles long ago
Heard it on the Aegean, and it brought
Into his mind the turbid ebb and flow
Of human misery: we
Find also in the sound a thought,
Hearing it by this distant northern sea.

strand] beach
tremulous] quivering
cadence] rhythm
Sophocles] Ancient Greek tragedian
Aegean] i.e. the Aegean Sea (east of Greece)
turbid] muddy, unclear, confused

The Sea of Faith
Was once, too, at the full, and round earth's shore
Lay like folds of a bright girdle furled.
But now I only hear
Its melancholy, long, withdrawing roar,
Retreating, to the breath
Of the night-wind, down the vast edges drear
And naked shingles of the world.

Ah, love, let us be true
To one another! for the world, which seems
To lie before us like a land of dreams,
So various, so beautiful, so new,
Hath really neither joy, nor love, nor light,
Nor certitude, nor peace, nor help for pain;
And we are here as on a darkling plain
Swept with confused alarms of struggle and flight,
Where ignorant armies clash by night.

darkling] shadowy, obscure, dark

99

Amends

ADRIENNE RICH

Nights like this: on the cold apple-bough
a white star, then another
exploding out of the bark:
on the ground, moonlight picking at small stones

as it picks at greater stones, as it rises with the surf
laying its cheek for moments on the sand
as it licks the broken ledge, as it flows up the cliffs,
as it flicks across the tracks

as it unavailing pours into the gash
of the sand-and-gravel quarry
as it leans across the hangared fuselage
of the crop-dusting plane

as it soaks through cracks into the trailers
tremulous with sleep
as it dwells upon the eyelids of the sleepers
as if to make amends

hangared] inside a hangar
fuselage] the body of an aeroplane
tremulous] quivering

100

Full Moon and Little Frieda

TED HUGHES

A cool small evening shrunk to a dog bark and the clank
     of a bucket –

And you listening.
A spider's web, tense for the dew's touch.
A pail lifted, still and brimming – mirror
To tempt a first star to a tremor.

Cows are going home in the lane there, looping the
     hedges with their warm wreaths of breath –
A dark river of blood, many boulders,
Balancing unspilled milk.

'Moon!' you cry suddenly, 'Moon! Moon!'

The moon has stepped back like an artist gazing amazed
     at a work

That points at him amazed.

101

Lament

GILLIAN CLARKE

For the green turtle with her pulsing burden,
in search of the breeding-ground.
For her eggs laid in their nest of sickness.

For the cormorant in his funeral silk,
the veil of iridescence on the sand,
the shadow on the sea.

For the ocean's lap with its mortal stain.
For Ahmed at the closed border.
For the soldier in his uniform of fire.

For the gunsmith and the armourer,
the boy fusilier who joined for the company,
the farmer's sons, in it for the music.

For the hook-beaked turtles,
the dugong and the dolphin,
the whale struck dumb by the missile's thunder.

For the tern, the gull and the restless wader,
the long migrations and the slow dying,
the veiled sun and the stink of anger.

For the burnt earth and the sun put out,
the scalded ocean and the blazing well.
For vengeance, and the ashes of language.

cormorant . . . tern . . . gull . . . wader] types of seabirds
iridescence] a surface of shimmering colours
fusilier] rifleman
dugong] large aquatic mammal

102

On The Grasshopper and The Cricket

JOHN KEATS

The poetry of earth is never dead:
    When all the birds are faint with the hot sun,
    And hide in cooling trees, a voice will run
From hedge to hedge about the new-mown mead;
That is the grasshopper's – he takes the lead
    In summer luxury, – he has never done
    With his delights; for when tired out with fun
He rests at ease beneath some pleasant weed.
The poetry of earth is ceasing never:
    On a lone winter evening, when the frost
        Has wrought a silence, from the stove there shrills
The cricket's song, in warmth increasing ever,
    And seems to one in drowsiness half lost,
        The grasshopper's among some grassy hills.

mead] meadow

103

The Flower-Fed Buffaloes

VACHEL LINDSAY

The flower-fed buffaloes of the spring
In the days of long ago,
Ranged where the locomotives sing
And the prairie flowers lie low:–
The tossing, blooming, perfumed grass
Is swept away by the wheat,
Wheels and wheels and wheels spin by
In the spring that still is sweet.
But the flower-fed buffaloes of the spring
Left us, long ago.
They gore no more, they bellow no more,
They trundle around the hills no more:–
With the Blackfeet, lying low,
With the Pawnees, lying low,
Lying low.

Blackfeet . . . Pawnees] Native American tribes

104

Report To Wordsworth

BOEY KIM CHENG

You should be here, Nature has need of you.
She has been laid waste. Smothered by the smog,
the flowers are mute, and the birds are few
in a sky slowing like a dying clock.
All hopes of Proteus rising from the sea
have sunk; he is entombed in the waste
we dump. Triton's notes struggle to be free,
his famous horns are choked, his eyes are dazed,
and Neptune lies helpless as a beached whale,
while insatiate man moves in for the kill.
Poetry and piety have begun to fail,
as Nature's mighty heart is lying still.
O see the wound widening in the sky,
God is labouring to utter his last cry.

Wordsworth] i.e. the English nature-poet William Wordsworth (1770–1850)
Proteus] (Greek mythology) a shape-changing sea-god
Triton] (Greek mythology) a sea-god that used shells as wind instruments
Neptune] the Roman god of the sea
insatiate] never satisfied

105

First Love

JOHN CLARE

I ne'er was struck before that hour
     With love so sudden and so sweet
Her face it bloomed like a sweet flower
     And stole my heart away complete
My face turned pale a deadly pale
     My legs refused to walk away
And when she looked what could I ail
My life and all seemed turned to clay

And then my blood rushed to my face
     And took my eyesight quite away
The trees and bushes round the place
     Seemed midnight at noon day
I could not see a single thing
     Words from my eyes did start
They spoke as chords do from the string
     And blood burnt round my heart

Are flowers the winters choice
     Is love's bed always snow
She seemed to hear my silent voice
     Not loves appeals to know
I never saw so sweet a face
     As that I stood before
My heart has left its dwelling place
     And can return no more –

what could I ail] what could be wrong

106

Marrysong

DENNIS SCOTT

He never learned her, quite. Year after year
that territory, without seasons, shifted
under his eye. An hour he could be lost
in the walled anger of her quarried hurt
on turning, see cool water laughing where
the day before there were stones in her voice.
He charted. She made wilderness again.
Roads disappeared. The map was never true.
Wind brought him rain sometimes, tasting of sea –
and suddenly she would change the shape of shores
faultlessly calm. All, all was each day new;
the shadows of her love shortened or grew
like trees seen from an unexpected hill,
new country at each jaunty helpless journey.
So he accepted that geography, constantly strange.
Wondered. Stayed home increasingly to find
his way among the landscapes of her mind.

charted] mapped

107

So, We'll Go No More A-Roving

GEORGE GORDON, LORD BYRON

So, we'll go no more a-roving
    So late into the night,
Though the heart be still as loving,
    And the moon be still as bright.

For the sword outwears its sheath,
    And the soul wears out the breast,
And the heart must pause to breathe,
    And love itself have rest.

Though the night was made for loving,
    And the day returns too soon,
Yet we'll go no more a-roving
    By the light of the moon.

108

Sonnet 43

ELIZABETH BARRETT BROWNING

How do I love thee? Let me count the ways! –
I love thee to the depth & breadth & height
My soul can reach, when feeling out of sight
For the ends of Being and Ideal Grace.
I love thee to the level of everyday's
Most quiet need, by sun & candlelight –
I love thee freely, as men strive for Right, –
I love thee purely, as they turn from Praise;
I love thee with the passion, put to use
In my old griefs, . . and with my childhood's faith:
I love thee with the love I seemed to lose
With my lost Saints, – I love thee with the breath,
Smiles, tears, of all my life! – and, if God choose,
I shall but love thee better after my death.

109

Sonnet 29

EDNA ST VINCENT MILLAY

Pity me not because the light of day
At close of day no longer walks the sky;
Pity me not for beauties passed away
From field to thicket as the year goes by;
Pity me not the waning of the moon,
Nor that the ebbing tide goes out to sea,
Nor that a man's desire is hushed so soon,
And you no longer look with love on me.
This have I known always: Love is no more
Than the wide blossom which the wind assails,
Than the great tide that treads the shifting shore,
Strewing fresh wreckage gathered in the gales:
Pity me that the heart is slow to learn
When the swift mind beholds at every turn.

Part 4

*Poems from the Nineteenth
and Twentieth Centuries (II)*

110

A Different History

SUJATA BHATT

Great Pan is not dead;
he simply emigrated
        to India.
Here, the gods roam freely,
disguised as snakes or monkeys;
every tree is sacred
and it is a sin
to be rude to a book.
It is a sin to shove a book aside
                with your foot,
a sin to slam books down
        hard on a table,
a sin to toss one carelessly
        across a room.
You must learn how to turn the pages gently
without disturbing Sarasvati,
without offending the tree
from whose wood the paper was made.

        Which language
        has not been the oppressor's tongue?
        Which language
        truly meant to murder someone?
        And how does it happen
        that after the torture,
        after the soul has been cropped
        with a long scythe swooping out
        of the conqueror's face –
        the unborn grandchildren
        grow to love that strange language.

Pan] the Ancient Greek god of nature, part-man, part-goat
Sarasvati] the Hindu goddess of the arts

111

Pied Beauty

GERARD MANLEY HOPKINS

Glory be to God for dappled things –
    For skies of couple-colour as a brinded cow;
        For rose-moles all in stipple upon trout that swim;
Fresh-firecoal chestnut-falls; finches' wings;
    Landscape plotted and pieced – fold, fallow, and plough;
        And all trades, their gear and tackle and trim.
All things counter, original, spare, strange;
    Whatever is fickle, freckled (who knows how?)
        With swift, slow; sweet, sour; adazzle, dim;
He fathers-forth whose beauty is past change:
        Praise him.

pied . . . dappled . . . couple-colour] of different shades of colour; two-tone
brinded] streaked with different colours
fresh-firecoal chestnut-falls] falling chestnuts as bright as glowing coals
counter] opposite, duplicate
fathers-forth] creates, engenders

112

Continuum

ALLEN CURNOW

The moon rolls over the roof and falls behind
my house, and the moon does neither of these things,
I am talking about myself.

It's not possible to get off to sleep or
the subject or the planet, nor to think thoughts.
Better barefoot it out the front

door and lean from the porch across the privets
and the palms into the washed-out creation,
a dark place with two particular

bright clouds dusted (query) by the moon, one's mine
the other's an adversary, which may depend
on the wind, or something.

A long moment stretches, the next one is not
on time. Not unaccountably the chill of
the planking underfoot rises

in the throat, for its part the night sky empties
the whole of its contents down. Turn on a bare
heel, close the door behind

on the author, cringing demiurge, who picks up
his litter and his tools and paces me back
to bed, stealthily in step.

continuum] that which extends continuously
privets] hedges
demiurge] creator

113

Horses

EDWIN MUIR

Those lumbering horses in the steady plough,
On the bare field – I wonder why, just now,
They seemed terrible, so wild and strange,
Like magic power on the stony grange.

Perhaps some childish hour has come again,
When I watched fearful, through the blackening rain,
Their hooves like pistons in an ancient mill
Move up and down, yet seem as standing still.

Their conquering hooves which trod the stubble down
Were ritual that turned the field to brown,
And their great hulks were seraphim of gold,
Or mute ecstatic monsters on the mould.

And oh the rapture, when, one furrow done,
They marched broad-breasted to the sinking sun!
The light flowed off their bossy sides in flakes;
The furrows rolled behind like struggling snakes.

But when at dusk with steaming nostrils home
They came, they seemed gigantic in the gloam,
And warm and glowing with mysterious fire
That lit their smouldering bodies in the mire.

grange] farmhouse
seraphim] angels
mould] ground
bossy] swelling
gloam] dusk
mire] mud

Their eyes as brilliant and as wide as night
Gleamed with a cruel apocalyptic light.
Their manes the leaping ire of the wind
Lifted with rage invisible and blind.

Ah, now it fades! It fades! and I must pine
Again for that dread country crystalline,
Where the black field and the still-standing tree
Were bright and fearful presences to me.

crystalline] as if made of crystal

114

Hunting Snake

JUDITH WRIGHT

Sun-warmed in this late season's grace
under the autumn's gentlest sky
we walked, and froze half-through a pace.
The great black snake went reeling by.

Head-down, tongue flickering on the trail
he quested through the parting grass;
sun glazed his curves of diamond scale,
and we lost breath to watch him pass.

What track he followed, what small food
fled living from his fierce intent,
we scarcely thought; still as we stood
our eyes went with him as he went.

Cold, dark and splendid he was gone
into the grass that hid his prey.
We took a deeper breath of day,
looked at each other, and went on.

115

Pike

TED HUGHES

Pike, three inches long, perfect
Pike in all parts, green tigering the gold.
Killers from the egg: the malevolent aged grin.
They dance on the surface among the flies.

Or move, stunned by their own grandeur
Over a bed of emerald, silhouette
Of submarine delicacy and horror.
A hundred feet long in their world.

In ponds, under the heat-struck lily pads –
Gloom of their stillness:
Logged on last year's black leaves, watching upwards.
Or hung in an amber cavern of weeds

The jaws' hooked clamp and fangs
Not to be changed at this date;
A life subdued to its instrument;
The gills kneading quietly, and the pectorals.

Three we kept behind glass,
Jungled in weed: three inches, four,
And four and a half: fed fry to them –
Suddenly there were two. Finally one.

Pike] large, predatory freshwater fish
tigering] i.e. making stripes like a tiger's skin
pectorals] lateral fins
fry] newly hatched fish

With a sag belly and the grin it was born with.
And indeed they spare nobody.
Two, six pounds each, over two feet long,
High and dry and dead in the willow-herb –

One jammed past its gills down the other's gullet:
The outside eye stared: as a vice locks –
The same iron in this eye
Though its film shrank in death.

A pond I fished, fifty years across,
Whose lilies and muscular tench
Had outlasted every visible stone
Of the monastery that planted them –

Stilled legendary depth:
It was as deep as England. It held
Pike too immense to stir, so immense and old
That past nightfall I dared not cast

But silently cast and fished
With the hair frozen on my head
For what might move, for what eye might move.
The still splashes on the dark pond,

Owls hushing the floating woods
Frail on my ear against the dream
Darkness beneath night's darkness had freed,
That rose slowly towards me, watching.

willow-herb] yellow loosestrife, a wild plant
film] the eye's surface
tench] freshwater fish
cast] flick the line of a fishing-rod

116

A Birthday

CHRISTINA ROSSETTI

My heart is like a singing bird
    Whose nest is in a watered shoot;
My heart is like an apple-tree
    Whose boughs are bent with thickset fruit;
My heart is like a rainbow shell
    That paddles in a halcyon sea;
My heart is gladder than all these
    Because my love is come to me.

Raise me a dais of silk and down;
    Hang it with vair and purple dyes;
Carve it in doves and pomegranates,
    And peacocks with a hundred eyes;
Work it in gold and silver grapes,
    In leaves and silver fleurs-de-lys;
Because the birthday of my life
    Is come, my love is come to me.

halcyon] idyllic, calm
dais] platform
down] soft feathers
vair] squirrel fur
eyes] i.e. the circles in a peacock's tail
fleurs-de-lys] three-petalled flowers

117

The Woodspurge

DANTE GABRIEL ROSSETTI

The wind flapped loose, the wind was still,
Shaken out dead from tree and hill:
I had walked on at the wind's will, –
I sat now, for the wind was still.

Between my knees my forehead was, –
My lips, drawn in, said not Alas!
My hair was over in the grass,
My naked ears heard the day pass.

My eyes, wide open, had the run
Of some ten weeds to fix upon;
Among those few, out of the sun,
The woodspurge flowered, three cups in one.

From perfect grief there need not be
Wisdom or even memory:
One thing then learnt remains to me, –
The woodspurge has a cup of three.

at the wind's will] wherever the wind blew me
Woodspurge] a wild plant, whose flowers form in groups of three from a cup-like stem

118

The Cockroach

KEVIN HALLIGAN

I watched a giant cockroach start to pace,
Skirting a ball of dust that rode the floor.
At first he seemed quite satisfied to trace
A path between the wainscot and the door,
But soon he turned to jog in crooked rings,
Circling the rusty table leg and back,
And flipping right over to scratch his wings –
As if the victim of a mild attack
Of restlessness that worsened over time.
After a while, he climbed an open shelf
And stopped. He looked uncertain where to go.
Was this due payment for some vicious crime
A former life had led to? I don't know,
Except I thought I recognised myself.

skirting] avoiding by a detour
wainscot] panelling

119

The City Planners

MARGARET ATWOOD

Cruising these residential Sunday
streets in dry August sunlight:
what offends us is
the sanities:
the houses in pedantic rows, the planted
sanitary trees, assert
levelness of surface like a rebuke
to the dent in our car door.
No shouting here, or
shatter of glass; nothing more abrupt
than the rational whine of a power mower
cutting a straight swath in the discouraged grass.

But though the driveways neatly
sidestep hysteria
by being even, the roofs all display
the same slant of avoidance to the hot sky,
certain things:
the smell of spilt oil a faint
sickness lingering in the garages,
a splash of paint on brick surprising as a bruise,
a plastic hose poised in a vicious
coil; even the too-fixed stare of the wide windows

give momentary access to
the landscape behind or under
the future cracks in the plaster

sanities] *sanity* = the condition of mental health
swath] track, row

when the houses, capsized, will slide
obliquely into the clay seas, gradual as glaciers
that right now nobody notices.

That is where the City Planners
with the insane faces of political conspirators
are scattered over unsurveyed
territories, concealed from each other,
each in his own private blizzard;

guessing directions, they sketch
transitory lines rigid as wooden borders
on a wall in the white vanishing air

tracing the panic of suburb
order in a bland madness of snows.

120

The Planners

BOEY KIM CHENG

They plan. They build. All spaces are gridded,
filled with permutations of possibilities.
The buildings are in alignment with the roads
which meet at desired points
linked by bridges all hang
in the grace of mathematics.
They build and will not stop.
Even the sea draws back
and the skies surrender.

They erase the flaws,
the blemishes of the past, knock off
useless blocks with dental dexterity.
All gaps are plugged
with gleaming gold.
The country wears perfect rows
of shining teeth.
Anaesthesia, amnesia, hypnosis.
They have the means.
They have it all so it will not hurt,
so history is new again.
The piling will not stop.
The drilling goes right through
the fossils of last century.

But my heart would not bleed
poetry. Not a single drop
to stain the blueprint
of our past's tomorrow.

piling] building foundations
blueprint] architectural plan

121

Summer Farm

NORMAN MacCAIG

Straws like tame lightnings lie about the grass
And hang zigzag on hedges. Green as glass
The water in the horse-trough shines.
Nine ducks go wobbling by in two straight lines.

A hen stares at nothing with one eye,
Then picks it up. Out of an empty sky
A swallow falls and, flickering through
The barn, dives up again into the dizzy blue.

I lie, not thinking, in the cool, soft grass,
Afraid of where a thought might take me – as
This grasshopper with plated face
Unfolds his legs and finds himself in space.

Self under self, a pile of selves I stand
Threaded on time, and with metaphysic hand
Lift the farm like a lid and see
Farm within farm, and in the centre, me.

plated] i.e. as if comprising sections of metal plate
metaphysic] concerned with the nature of abstract or transcendent truth

122

Where I Come From

ELIZABETH BREWSTER

People are made of places. They carry with them
hints of jungles or mountains, a tropic grace
or the cool eyes of sea-gazers. Atmosphere of cities
how different drops from them, like the smell of smog
or the almost-not-smell of tulips in the spring,
nature tidily plotted in little squares
with a fountain in the centre; museum smell,
art also tidily plotted with a guidebook;
or the smell of work, glue factories maybe,
chromium-plated offices; smell of subways
crowded at rush hours.

                    Where I come from, people
carry woods in their minds, acres of pine woods;
blueberry patches in the burned-out bush;
wooden farmhouses, old, in need of paint,
with yards where hens and chickens circle about,
clucking aimlessly; battered schoolhouses
behind which violets grow. Spring and winter
are the mind's chief seasons: ice and the breaking of ice.

A door in the mind blows open, and there blows
a frosty wind from fields of snow.

123

Sonnet: Composed Upon Westminster Bridge

WILLIAM WORDSWORTH

Earth has not anything to show more fair:
Dull would he be of soul who could pass by
A sight so touching in its majesty:
This City now doth like a garment wear
The beauty of the morning; silent, bare,
Ships, towers, domes, theatres, and temples lie
Open unto the fields, and to the sky;
All bright and glittering in the smokeless air.
Never did sun more beautifully steep
In his first splendour, valley, rock, or hill;
Ne'er saw I, never felt, a calm so deep!
The river glideth at his own sweet will:
Dear God! the very houses seem asleep;
And all that mighty heart is lying still!

Westminster Bridge] i.e. across the River Thames in London
steep] bathe (in light)
glideth] glides

124

The Bay

JAMES K. BAXTER

On the road to the bay was a lake of rushes
Where we bathed at times and changed in the bamboos.
Now it is rather to stand and say:
How many roads we take that lead to Nowhere,
The alley overgrown, no meaning now but loss:
Not that veritable garden where everything comes easy.

And by the bay itself were cliffs with carved names
And a hut on the shore beside the Maori ovens.
We raced boats from the banks of the pumice creek
Or swam in those autumnal shallows
Growing cold in amber water, riding the logs
Upstream, and waiting for the taniwha.

So now I remember the bay and the little spiders
On driftwood, so poisonous and quick.
The carved cliffs and the great outcrying surf
With currents round the rocks and the birds rising.
A thousand times an hour is torn across
And burned for the sake of going on living.
But I remember the bay that never was
And stand like stone and cannot turn away.

taniwha] a sea monster in Maori mythology

125

Where Lies the Land?

ARTHUR HUGH CLOUGH

Where lies the land to which the ship would go?
Far, far ahead, is all her seamen know.
And where the land she travels from? Away,
Far, far behind, is all that they can say.

On sunny noons upon the deck's smooth face,
Linked arm in arm, how pleasant here to pace!
Or, o'er the stern reclining, watch below
The foaming wake far widening as we go.

On stormy nights when wild north-westers rave,
How proud a thing to fight with wind and wave!
The dripping sailor on the reeling mast
Exults to bear and scorns to wish it past.

Where lies the land to which the ship would go?
Far, far ahead, is all her seamen know.
And where the land she travels from? Away,
Far, far behind, is all that they can say.

stern] the rear part of a ship
wake] the trace left in the sea by a ship's passage
north-westers] violent gales
Exults to] relishes the opportunity to

126

Morse

LES MURRAY

Tuckett. Bill Tuckett. Telegraph operator, Hall's Creek
which is way out back of the Outback, but he stuck it,
quite likely liked it, despite heat, glare, dust and the lack
of diversion or doctors. Come disaster you trusted to luck,
ingenuity and pluck. This was back when nice people said pluck,
the sleevelink and green eyeshade epoch.
                              Faced, though, like Bill Tuckett
with a man needing surgery right on the spot, a lot
would have done their dashes. It looked hopeless (dot dot dot)
Lift him up on the table, said Tuckett, running the key hot
till Head Office turned up a doctor who coolly instructed
up a thousand miles of wire, as Tuckett advanced slit by slit
with a safety razor blade, pioneering on into the wet,
copper-wiring the rivers off, in the first operation conducted
along dotted lines, with rum drinkers gripping the patient:
d-d-dash it, take care, Tuck!
                              And the vital spark stayed unshorted.
Yallah! Breathed the camelmen. Tuckett, you did it, you did it!
cried the spattered la-de-dah jodhpur-wearing Inspector of Stock.
We imagine, some weeks later, a properly laconic
convalescent averring Without you, I'd have kicked the bucket . . .
From Chungking to Burrenjuck, morse keys have mostly gone silent
and only old men meet now to chit-chat in their electric
bygone dialect. The last letter many will forget
is dit-dit-dit-dah, V for Victory. The coders' hero had speed,
resource and a touch. So ditditdit daah for Bill Tuckett.

Morse] the system of electric communication, invented by Samuel Morse, by which the letters of the
    alphabet were rendered as a series of short ('dots' or 'dit') or long ('dashes' or 'dah') transmissions
Outback] the Australian interior
unshorted] with no short-circuits
la-de-dah] using affectedly upper-class speech and manners

127

The Man with Night Sweats

THOM GUNN

I wake up cold, I who
Prospered through dreams of heat
Wake to their residue,
Sweat, and a clinging sheet.

My flesh was its own shield:
Where it was gashed, it healed.

I grew as I explored
The body I could trust
Even while I adored
The risk that made robust,

A world of wonders in
Each challenge to the skin.

I cannot but be sorry
The given shield was cracked
My mind reduced to hurry,
My flesh reduced and wrecked.

I have to change the bed,
But catch myself instead

Stopped upright where I am
Hugging my body to me
As if to shield it from
The pains that will go through me,

As if hands were enough
To hold an avalanche off.

128

Night Sweat

ROBERT LOWELL

Work-table, litter, books and standing lamp,
plain things, my stalled equipment, the old broom –
but I am living in a tidied room,
for ten nights now I've felt the creeping damp
float over my pajamas' wilted white . . .
Sweet salt embalms me and my head is wet,
everything streams and tells me this is right;
my life's fever is soaking in night sweat –
one life, one writing! But the downward glide
and bias of existing wrings us dry –
always inside me is the child who died,
always inside me is his will to die –
one universe, one body . . . in this urn
the animal night sweats of the spirit burn.
Behind me! You! Again I feel the light
lighten my leaded eyelids, while the gray
skulled horses whinny for the soot of night.
I dabble in the dapple of the day,
a heap of wet clothes, seamy, shivering,
I see my flesh and bedding washed with light,
my child exploding into dynamite,
my wife . . . your lightness alters everything,
and tears the black web from the spider's sack,
as your heart hops and flutters like a hare.
Poor turtle, tortoise, if I cannot clear
the surface of these troubled waters here,
absolve me, help me, Dear Heart, as you bear
this world's dead weight and cycle on your back.

129

Rain

EDWARD THOMAS

Rain, midnight rain, nothing but the wild rain
On this bleak hut, and solitude, and me
Remembering again that I shall die
And neither hear the rain nor give it thanks
For washing me cleaner than I have been
Since I was born into this solitude.
Blessed are the dead that the rain rains upon:
But here I pray that none whom once I loved
Is dying to-night or lying still awake
Solitary, listening to the rain,
Either in pain or thus in sympathy
Helpless among the living and the dead,
Like a cold water among broken reeds,
Myriads of broken reeds all still and stiff,
Like me who have no love which this wild rain
Has not dissolved except the love of death,
If love it be for what is perfect and
Cannot, the tempest tells me, disappoint.

130

Any Soul to Any Body

COSMO MONKHOUSE

So we must part, my body, you and I
          Who've spent so many pleasant years together.
'Tis sorry work to lose your company
          Who clove to me so close, whate'er the weather,
From winter unto winter, wet or dry;
          But you have reached the limit of your tether,
And I must journey on my way alone,
And leave you quietly beneath a stone.

They say that you are altogether bad
          (Forgive me, 'tis not my experience),
And think me very wicked to be sad
          At leaving you, a clod, a prison, whence
To get quite free I should be very glad.
          Perhaps I may be so, some few days hence,
But now, methinks, 'twere graceless not to spend
A tear or two on my departing friend.

Now our long partnership is near completed,
          And I look back upon its history;
I greatly fear I have not always treated
          You with the honesty you showed to me.
And I must own that you have oft defeated
          Unworthy schemes by your sincerity,
And by a blush or stammering tongue have tried
To make me think again before I lied.

sorry work] a sad business
clove to] cleaved to, hugged
clod] shapeless lump of earth (from which the body is fashioned)

'Tis true you're not so handsome as you were,
    But that's not your fault and is partly mine.
You might have lasted longer with more care,
    And still looked something like your first design;
And even now, with all your wear and tear,
    'Tis pitiful to think I must resign
You to the friendless grave, the patient prey
Of all the hungry legions of Decay.

But you must stay, dear body, and I go.
    And I was once so very proud of you:
You made my mother's eyes to overflow
    When first she saw you, wonderful and new.
And now, with all your faults, 'twere hard to find
    A slave more willing or a friend more true.
Ay – even they who say the worst about you
Can scarcely tell what I shall do without you.

legions] armies

131

The Spirit is too Blunt an Instrument

ANNE STEVENSON

The spirit is too blunt an instrument
to have made this baby.
Nothing so unskilful as human passions
could have managed the intricate
exacting particulars: the tiny
blind bones with their manipulating tendons,
the knee and the knucklebones, the resilient
fine meshings of ganglia and vertebrae,
the chain of the difficult spine.

Observe the distinct eyelashes and sharp crescent
fingernails, the shell-like complexity
of the ear, with its firm involutions
concentric in miniature to minute
ossicles. Imagine the
infinitesimal capillaries, the flawless connections
of the lungs, the invisible neural filaments
through which the completed body
already answers to the brain.

ganglia] bunches of nerve-endings
involutions] curled structures
ossicles] small bones
infinitesimal] most tiny
capillaries] fine blood-vessels
neural] of nerves
filaments] threads

Then name any passion or sentiment
possessed of the simplest accuracy.
No, no desire or affection could have done
with practice what habit
has done perfectly, indifferently,
through the body's ignorant precision.
It is left to the vagaries of the mind to invent
love and despair and anxiety
and their pain.

vagaries] capricious fluctuations

132

From *Long Distance*

TONY HARRISON

Though my mother was already two years dead
Dad kept her slippers warming by the gas,
put hot water bottles her side of the bed
and still went to renew her transport pass.

You couldn't just drop in. You had to phone.
He'd put you off an hour to give him time
to clear away her things and look alone
as though his still raw love were such a crime.

He couldn't risk my blight of disbelief
though sure that very soon he'd hear her key
scrape in the rusted lock and end his grief.
He *knew* she'd just popped out to get the tea.

I believe life ends with death, and that is all.
You haven't both gone shopping; just the same,
in my new black leather phone book there's your name
and the disconnected number I still call.

the gas] i.e. the gas-fire
transport pass] (old-person's) travel permit

133

From *Modern Love*

GEORGE MEREDITH

By this he knew she wept with waking eyes:
That, at his hand's light quiver by her head,
The strange low sobs that shook their common bed,
Were called into her with a sharp surprise,
And strangled mute, like little gasping snakes,
Dreadfully venomous to him. She lay
Stone-still, and the long darkness flowed away
With muffled pulses. Then, as midnight makes
Her giant heart of Memory and Tears
Drink the pale drug of silence, and so beat
Sleep's heavy measure, they from head to feet
Were moveless, looking through their dead black years,
By vain regret scrawled over the blank wall.
Like sculptured effigies they might be seen
Upon their marriage-tomb, the sword between;
Each wishing for the sword that severs all.

moveless] motionless
heavy measure] solemn rhythm
effigies] sculpted models

134

Funeral Blues

W.H. AUDEN

Stop all the clocks, cut off the telephone,
Prevent the dog from barking with a juicy bone,
Silence the pianos and with muffled drum
Bring out the coffin, let the mourners come.

Let aeroplanes circle moaning overhead
Scribbling on the sky the message He Is Dead,
Put crêpe bows round the white necks of the public doves,
Let the traffic policemen wear black cotton gloves.

He was my North, my South, my East and West,
My working week and my Sunday rest,
My noon, my midnight, my talk, my song;
I thought that love would last for ever: I was wrong.

The stars are not wanted now: put out every one;
Pack up the moon and dismantle the sun;
Pour away the ocean and sweep up the wood;
For nothing now can ever come to any good.

crêpe] thin crinkled fabric

135

La Figlia Che Piange

T.S. ELIOT

O quam te memorem virgo . . .

Stand on the highest pavement of the stair –
Lean on a garden urn –
Weave, weave the sunlight in your hair –
Clasp your flowers to you with a pained surprise –
Fling them to the ground and turn
With a fugitive resentment in your eyes:
But weave, weave the sunlight in your hair.

So I would have had him leave,
So I would have had her stand and grieve,
So he would have left
As the soul leaves the body torn and bruised,
As the mind deserts the body it has used.
I should find
Some way incomparably light and deft,
Some way we both should understand,
Simple and faithless as a smile and shake of the hand.

She turned away, but with the autumn weather
Compelled my imagination many days,
Many days and many hours:
Her hair over her arms and her arms full of flowers.
And I wonder how they should have been together!
I should have lost a gesture and a pose.
Sometimes these cogitations still amaze
The troubled midnight and the noon's repose.

La Figlia Che Piange] (Italian) the weeping girl
O quam te memorem virgo . . .] 'But by what name should I call thee, O maiden?' (Latin; from
  Virgil's *Aeneid*, addressed by Aeneas to his mother Venus, the goddess of love: the quotation
  continues, '. . . for thy face is not mortal')

136

From *Song of Myself*

WALT WHITMAN

I am the poet of the Body and I am the poet of the Soul,
The pleasures of heaven are with me and the pains of hell are with me,
The first I graft and increase upon myself, the latter I translate into a new tongue.

I am the poet of the woman the same as the man,
And I say it is as great to be a woman as to be a man,
And I say there is nothing greater than the mother of men.

I chant the chant of dilation or pride,
We have had ducking and deprecating about enough,
I show that size is only development.

Have you outstript the rest? are you the President?
It is a trifle, they will more than arrive there every one, and still pass on.
I am he that walks with the tender and growing night,
I call to the earth and sea half-held by the night.

Press close bare-bosom'd night – press close magnetic nourishing night!
Night of south winds – night of the large few stars
Still nodding night – mad naked summer night.

Smile O voluptuous cool-breath'd earth!
Earth of the slumbering and liquid trees!
Earth of departed sunset – earth of the mountains misty-topped!
Earth of the vitreous pour of the full moon just tinged with blue!

graft] transplant
dilation] expansion
vitreous] glassy

Earth of shine and dark mottling the tide of the river!
Earth of the limpid grey of clouds brighter and clearer for my sake!
Far-swooping elbowed earth – rich apple-blossom'd earth!
Smile, for your lover comes.
Prodigal, you have given me love – therefore I to you give love!
O unspeakable passionate love.

Prodigal] wastrel, reckless spendthrift

137

He Never Expected Much

THOMAS HARDY

Well, World, you have kept faith with me,
    Kept faith with me;
Upon the whole you have proved to be
    Much as you said you were.
Since as a child I used to lie
Upon the leaze and watch the sky,
Never, I own, expected I
    That life would all be fair.

'Twas then you said, and since have said,
    Times since have said,
In that mysterious voice you shed
    From clouds and hills around:
'Many have loved me desperately,
Many with smooth serenity,
While some have shown contempt of me
    Till they dropped underground.

'I do not promise overmuch,
    Child; overmuch;
Just neutral-tinted haps and such,'
    You said to minds like mine.
Wise warning for your credit's sake!
Which I for one failed not to take,
And hence could stem such strain and ache
    As each year might assign.

leaze] meadow-land
own] admit
haps] occurrences, chances
credit] belief
stem] curb, restrain

138

The Telephone Call

FLEUR ADCOCK

They asked me 'Are you sitting down?
Right? This is Universal Lotteries',
they said. 'You've won the top prize,
the Ultra-super Global Special.
What would you do with a million pounds?
Or, actually, with more than a million –
not that it makes a lot of difference
once you're a millionaire.' And they laughed.

'Are you OK?' they asked – 'Still there?
Come on, now, tell us, how does it feel?'
I said 'I just . . . I can't believe it!'
They said 'That's what they all say.
What else? Go on, tell us about it.'
I said 'I feel the top of my head
has floated off, out through the window,
revolving like a flying saucer.'

'That's unusual' they said. 'Go on.'
I said 'I'm finding it hard to talk.
My throat's gone dry, my nose is tingling.
I think I'm going to sneeze – or cry.'
'That's right' they said, 'don't be ashamed
of giving way to your emotions.
It isn't every day you hear
you're going to get a million pounds.

Relax, now, have a little cry;
we'll give you a moment . . .' 'Hang on!' I said.
'I haven't bought a lottery ticket
for years and years. And what did you say

the company's called?' They laughed again.
'Not to worry about a ticket.
We're Universal. We operate
A retrospective Chances Module.

Nearly everyone's bought a ticket
in some lottery or another,
once at least. We buy up the files,
feed the names into our computer,
and see who the lucky person is.'
'Well, that's incredible' I said.
'It's marvellous. I still can't quite . . .
I'll believe it when I see the cheque.'

'Oh,' they said, 'there's no cheque.'
'But the money?' 'We don't deal in money.
Experiences are what we deal in.
You've had a great experience, right?
Exciting? Something you'll remember?
That's your prize. So congratulations
from all of us at Universal.
Have a nice day!' And the line went dead.

139

A Consumer's Report

PETER PORTER

The name of the product I tested is *Life*,
I have completed the form you sent me ·
and understand that my answers are confidential.

I had it as a gift,
I didn't feel much while using it,
in fact I think I'd have liked to be more excited.
It seemed gentle on the hands
but left an embarrassing deposit behind.
It was not economical
and I have used much more than I thought
(I suppose I have about half left
but it's difficult to tell) –
although the instructions are fairly large
there are so many of them
I don't know which to follow, especially
as they seem to contradict each other.
I'm not sure such a thing
should be put in the way of children –
It's difficult to think of a purpose
Also the price is much too high.
Things are piling up so fast,
after all, the world got by
for a thousand million years
without this, do we need it now?
(Incidentally, please ask your man
to stop calling me 'the respondent',
I don't like the sound of it.)
There seems to be a lot of different labels,
sizes and colours should be uniform,
the shape is awkward, it's waterproof

but not heat resistant, it doesn't keep
yet it's very difficult to get rid of:
whenever they make it cheaper they seem
to put less in – if you say you don't
want it, then it's delivered anyway.
I'd agree it's a popular product,
it's got into the language; people
even say they're on the side of it.
Personally I think it's overdone,
a small thing people are ready
to behave badly about. I think
we should take it for granted. If its
experts are called philosophers or market
researchers or historians, we shouldn't
care. We are the consumers and the last
law makers. So finally, I'd buy it.
But the question of a 'best buy'
I'd like to leave until I get
the competitive product you said you'd send.

140

Request To A Year

JUDITH WRIGHT

If the year is meditating a suitable gift,
I should like it to be the attitude
of my great-great-grandmother,
legendary devotee of the arts,

who, having had eight children
and little opportunity for painting pictures,
sat one day on a high rock
beside a river in Switzerland

and from a difficult distance viewed
her second son, balanced on a small ice-floe,
drift down the current towards a waterfall
that struck rock-bottom eighty feet below,

while her second daughter, impeded,
no doubt, by the petticoats of the day,
stretched out a last-hope alpenstock
(which luckily later caught him on his way).

Nothing, it was evident, could be done;
and with the artist's isolating eye
my great-great-grandmother hastily sketched the scene.
The sketch survives to prove the story by.

Year, if you have no Mother's day present planned;
reach back and bring me the firmness of her hand.

ice-floe] sheet of floating ice
alpenstock] walking-staff

141

On Finding a Small Fly Crushed in a Book

CHARLES TENNYSON TURNER

Some hand, that never meant to do thee hurt,
Has crushed thee here between these pages pent;
But thou has left thine own fair monument,
Thy wings gleam out and tell me what thou wert:
Oh! that the memories, which survive us here,
Were half as lovely as these wings of thine!
Pure relics of a blameless life, that shine
Now thou art gone: Our doom is ever near:
The peril is beside us day by day;
The book will close upon us, it may be,
Just as we lift ourselves to soar away
Upon the summer-airs. But, unlike thee,
The closing book may stop our vital breath,
Yet leave no lustre on our page of death.

pent] shut up within

142

Ozymandias

PERCY BYSSHE SHELLEY

I met a traveller from an antique land
Who said: Two vast and trunkless legs of stone
Stand in the desert . . . Near them, on the sand,
Half sunk, a shattered visage lies, whose frown,
And wrinkled lip, and sneer of cold command,
Tell that its sculptor well those passions read
Which yet survive, stamped on these lifeless things,
The hand that mocked them, and the heart that fed:
And on the pedestal these words appear:
'My name is Ozymandias, king of kings:
Look on my works, ye Mighty, and despair!'
Nothing beside remains. Round the decay
Of that colossal wreck, boundless and bare
The lone and level sands stretch far away.

trunkless] lacking the chest or trunk of the body
stamped] inscribed

143

Away, Melancholy

STEVIE SMITH

Away, melancholy,
Away with it, let it go.

Are not the trees green,
The earth as green?
Does not the wind blow,
Fire leap and the rivers flow?
Away melancholy.

The ant is busy
He carrieth his meat,
All things hurry
To be eaten or eat.
Away, melancholy.

Man, too, hurries,
Eats, couples, buries,
He is an animal also
With a hey ho melancholy,
Away with it, let it go.

Man of all creatures
Is superlative
(Away melancholy)
He of all creatures alone
Raiseth a stone
(Away melancholy)
Into the stone, the god
Pours what he knows of good
Calling, good, God.
Away melancholy, let it go.

Speak not to me of tears,
Tyranny, pox, wars,
Saying, Can God
Stone of man's thought, be good?

Say rather it is enough
That the stuffed
Stone of man's good, growing,
By man's called God.
Away, melancholy, let it go.

Man aspires
To good,
To love
Sighs;

Beaten, corrupted, dying
In his own blood lying
Yet heaves up an eye above
Cries, Love, love.
It is his virtue needs explaining,
Not his failing.

Away, melancholy,
Away with it, let it go.

Part 5

*Poems from the Nineteenth
and Twentieth Centuries (III)*

144

Childhood

FRANCES CORNFORD

I used to think that grown-up people chose
To have stiff backs and wrinkles round their nose,
And veins like small fat snakes on either hand,
On purpose to be grand.
Till through the banisters I watched one day
My great-aunt Etty's friend who was going away,
And how her onyx beads had come unstrung.
I saw her grope to find them as they rolled;
And then I knew that she was helplessly old,
As I was helplessly young.

onyx] a semi-precious stone

145

Because I Could Not Stop For Death

EMILY DICKINSON

Because I could not stop for Death —
He kindly stopped for me —
The Carriage held but just Ourselves —
And Immortality.

We slowly drove — He knew no haste
And I had put away
My labor and my leisure too,
For his Civility —

We passed the School, where Children strove
At Recess — in the Ring —
We passed the Fields of Gazing Grain —
We passed the Setting Sun —

Or rather — He passed Us —
The Dews drew quivering and chill —
For only Gossamer, my Gown —
My Tippet — only Tulle —

We paused before a House that seemed
A Swelling of the Ground —
The Roof was scarcely visible —
The Cornice — in the Ground —

Since then — 'tis Centuries — and yet
Feels shorter than the Day
I first surmised the Horses' Heads
Were toward Eternity —

Tippet] narrow scarf
Tulle] finely spun silk gauze
Cornice] decorative ceiling ornament

146

One Art

ELIZABETH BISHOP

The art of losing isn't hard to master;
so many things seem filled with the intent
to be lost that their loss is no disaster.

Lose something every day. Accept the fluster
of lost door keys, the hour badly spent.
The art of losing isn't hard to master.

Then practice losing farther, losing faster:
places, and names, and where it was you meant
to travel. None of these will bring disaster.

I lost my mother's watch. And look! my last, or
next-to-last, of three loved houses went.
The art of losing isn't hard to master.

I lost two cities, lovely ones. And, vaster,
some realms I owned, two rivers, a continent.
I miss them, but it wasn't a disaster.

– Even losing you (the joking voice, a gesture
I love) I shan't have lied. It's evident
the art of losing's not too hard to master
though it may look like (*Write* it!) like disaster.

147

Song: *Tears, Idle Tears*

ALFRED, LORD TENNYSON

Tears, idle tears, I know not what they mean,
Tears from the depth of some divine despair
Rise in the heart, and gather to the eyes,
In looking on the happy Autumn-fields,
And thinking of the days that are no more.

Fresh as the first beam glittering on a sail,
That brings our friends up from the underworld,
Sad as the last which reddens over one
That sinks with all we love below the verge;
So sad, so fresh, the days that are no more.

Ah, sad and strange as in dark summer dawns
The earliest pipe of half-awakened birds
To dying ears, when unto dying eyes
The casement slowly grows a glimmering square;
So sad, so strange, the days that are no more.

Dear as remembered kisses after death,
And sweet as those by hopeless fancy feigned
On lips that are for others; deep as love,
Deep as first love, and wild with all regret;
O Death in Life, the days that are no more.

pipe] song
casement] window

148

My Parents

STEPHEN SPENDER

My parents kept me from children who were rough
Who threw words like stones and wore torn clothes
Their thighs showed through rags. They ran in the street
And climbed cliffs and tripped by the country streams.

I feared more than tigers their muscles like iron
Their jerking hands and their knees tight on my arms
I feared the salt coarse pointing of those boys
Who copied my lisp behind me on the road.

They were lithe, they sprang out behind hedges
Like dogs to bark at my world. They threw mud
While I looked the other way, pretending to smile.
I longed to forgive them but they never smiled.

149

For Heidi With Blue Hair

FLEUR ADCOCK

When you dyed your hair blue
(or, at least, ultramarine
for the clipped sides, with a crest
of jet-black spikes on top)
you were sent home from school

because, as the headmistress put it,
although dyed hair was not
specifically forbidden, yours
was, apart from anything else,
not done in the school colours.

Tears in the kitchen, telephone-calls
to school from your freedom-loving father:
'She's not a punk in her behaviour;
it's just a style.' (You wiped your eyes,
also not in a school colour.)

'She discussed it with me first –
we checked the rules.' 'And anyway, Dad,
it cost twenty-five dollars.
Tell them it won't wash out –
not even if I wanted to try.'

It would have been unfair to mention
your mother's death, but that
shimmered behind the arguments.
The school had nothing else against you;
the teachers twittered and gave in.

punk] a teenage fashion and music style of the 1970s

Next day your black friend had hers done
in grey, white and flaxen yellow –
the school colours precisely:
an act of solidarity, a witty
tease. The battle was already won.

150

Praise Song For My Mother

GRACE NICHOLS

You were
water to me
deep and bold and fathoming

You were
moon's eye to me
pull and grained and mantling

You were
sunrise to me
rise and warm and streaming

You were
the fishes red gill to me
the flame tree's spread to me
the crab's leg/the fried plantain smell
                        replenishing replenishing

Go to your wide futures, you said

fathoming] (1) measuring a depth; (2) understanding
grained] seeded
mantling] enveloping, cushioning, surrounding

151

Follower

SEAMUS HEANEY

My father worked with a horse-plough,
His shoulders globed like a full sail strung
Between the shafts and the furrow.
The horses strained at his clicking tongue.

An expert. He would set the wing
And fit the bright steel-pointed sock.
The sod rolled over without breaking.
At the headrig, with a single pluck

Of reins, the sweating team turned round
And back into the land. His eye
Narrowed and angled at the ground,
Mapping the furrow exactly.

I stumbled in his hob-nailed wake,
Fell sometimes on the polished sod;
Sometimes he rode me on his back
Dipping and rising to his plod.

I wanted to grow up and plough,
To close one eye, stiffen my arm.
All I ever did was follow
In his broad shadow round the farm.

I was a nuisance, tripping, falling,
Yapping always. But today
It is my father who keeps stumbling
Behind me, and will not go away.

wing . . . sock . . . headrig] parts of the plough
yapping] chattering

152

Elegy For My Father's Father

JAMES K. BAXTER

He knew in the hour he died
That his heart had never spoken
In eighty years of days.
O for the tall tower broken
Memorial is denied:
And the unchanging cairn
That pipes could set ablaze
An aaronsrod and blossom.
They stood by the graveside
From his bitter veins born
And mourned him in their fashion.
A chain of sods in a day
He could slice and build
High as the head of a man
And a flowering cherry tree
On his walking shoulder held
Under the lion sun.
When he was old and blind
He sat in a curved chair
All day by the kitchen fire.
Many hours he had seen
The stars in their drunken dancing
Through the burning-glass of his mind
And sober knew the green
Boughs of heaven folding
The winter world in their hand.
The pride of his heart was dumb.

cairn] a pile of stones, raised as a monument
aaronsrod] flowering shrub
burning-glass] magnifying-glass

He knew in the hour he died
That his heart had never spoken
In song or bridal bed.
And the naked thought fell back
To a house by the waterside
And the leaves the wind had shaken
Then for a child's sake:
To the waves all night awake
With the dark mouths of the dead.
The tongues of water spoke
And his heart was unafraid.

153

The Trees Are Down

CHARLOTTE MEW

– and he cried with a loud voice:
Hurt not the earth, neither the sea, nor the trees – (Revelation)

They are cutting down the great plane-trees at the end of the garden.
    For days there has been the grate of the saw, the swish of the
        branches as they fall,
The crash of trunks, the rustle of trodden leaves,
With the 'Whoops' and the 'Whoas', the loud common talk, the
    loud common laughs of the men, above it all.

I remember one evening of a long past Spring
Turning in at a gate, getting out of a cart, and finding a large
    dead rat in the mud of the drive.
I remember thinking: alive or dead, a rat was a god-forsaken thing,
But at least, in May, that even a rat should be alive.
The week's work here is as good as done. There is just one bough
    On the roped bole, in the fine grey rain,
        Green and high
        And lonely against the sky.
        (Down now! –)
        And but for that,
        If an old dead rat
Did once, for a moment, unmake the Spring, I might never have
    thought of him again.

bole] tree-trunk

It is not for a moment the Spring is unmade to-day;
These were great trees, it was in them from root to stem:
When the men with the 'Whoops' and the 'Whoas' have carted
      the whole of the whispering loveliness away
Half the Spring, for me, will have gone with them.

It is going now, and my heart has been struck with the hearts of
      the planes;
Half my life it has beat with these, in the sun, in the rains,
          In the March wind, the May breeze,
In the great gales that came over to them across the roofs from
      the great seas.
          There was only a quiet rain when they were dying;
          They must have heard the sparrows flying,
And the small creeping creatures in the earth where they were lying –
          But I, all day, I heard an angel crying:
              'Hurt not the trees'.

154

The Trees

PHILIP LARKIN

The trees are coming into leaf
Like something almost being said;
The recent buds relax and spread,
Their greenness is a kind of grief.

Is it that they are born again
And we grow old? No, they die too.
Their yearly trick of looking new
Is written down in rings of grain.

Yet still the unresting castles thresh
In fullgrown thickness every May.
Last year is dead, they seem to say,
Begin afresh, afresh, afresh.

rings of grain] i.e. the yearly patterns within a log's cross-section

155

Country School

ALLEN CURNOW

You know the school; you call it old –
Scrub-worn floors and paint all peeled
On barge-board, weatherboard and gibbet belfry.

Pinus betrays, with rank tufts topping
The roof-ridge, scattering bravely
Nor'west gale as a reef its waves
While the small girls squeal at skipping
And magpies hoot from the eaves.

For scantling *Pinus* stands mature
In less than the life of a man;
The rusty saplings, the school, and you
Together your lives began.

O sweet antiquity! Look, the stone
That skinned your knees. How small
Are the terrible doors; how sad the dunny
And the things you drew on the wall.

gibbet] gallows
belfry] bell-tower
Pinus] (Latin) the botanical name for the pine-tree
rank] thickly growing
scantling] calibrating, measuring
dunny] (*slang*) toilet

156

Cambodia

JAMES FENTON

One man shall smile one day and say goodbye.
Two shall be left, two shall be left to die.

One man shall give his best advice.
Three men shall pay the price.

One man shall live, live to regret.
Four men shall meet the debt.

One man shall wake from terror to his bed.
Five men shall be dead.

One man to five. A million men to one.
And still they die. And still the war goes on.

157

Attack

SIEGFRIED SASSOON

At dawn the ridge emerges massed and dun
In the wild purple of the glowering sun,
Smouldering through spouts of drifting smoke that shroud
The menacing scarred slope; and, one by one,
Tanks creep and topple forward to the wire.
The barrage roars and lifts. Then, clumsily bowed
With bombs and guns and shovels and battle-gear,
Men jostle and climb to meet the bristling fire.
Lines of grey, muttering faces, masked with fear,
They leave their trenches, going over the top,
While time ticks blank and busy on their wrists,
And hope, with furtive eyes and grappling fists,
Flounders in mud. O Jesus, make it stop!

158

Reservist

BOEY KIM CHENG

Time again for the annual joust, the regular fanfare,
a call to arms, the imperative letters stern
as clarion notes, the king's command, upon
the pain of court-martial, to tilt
at the old windmills. With creaking bones
and suppressed grunts, we battle-weary knights
creep to attention, ransack the wardrobes
for our rusty armour, tuck the pot bellies
with great finesse into the shrinking gear,
and with helmets shutting off half our world,
report for service. We are again united
with sleek weapons we were betrothed to
in our active cavalier days.

We will keep charging up the same hills, plod
through the same forests, till we are too old,
too ill-fitted for life's other territories.
The same trails will find us time and again,
and we quick to obey, like children placed
on carousels they cannot get off from, borne
along through somebody's expensive fantasyland,
with an oncoming rush of tedious rituals, masked threats
and monsters armed with the same roar.

Reservist] a soldier serving within an auxiliary force as an emergency reserve
clarion] a war trumpet
tilt] joust with, charge on horseback towards (Cervantes's Don Quixote deludedly attacked
    windmills, thinking them enemy knights)
cavalier] knightly, breezy, youthful
carousels] merry-go-rounds

In the end we will perhaps surprise ourselves
and emerge unlikely heroes with long years
of braving the same horrors
pinned on our tunic fronts.
We will have proven that Sisyphus is not a myth.
We will play the game till the monotony
sends his lordship to sleep.
We will march the same paths till they break
onto new trails, our lives stumbling
onto the open sea, into daybreak.

Sisyphus] in Greek myth, the man condemned to push a boulder up a mountain, for ever

159

You Cannot Do This

GWENDOLYN MacEWEN

you cannot do this to them, these are my people;
I am not speaking of poetry, I am not speaking of art.
you cannot do this to them, these are my people.
you cannot hack away the horizon in front of their eyes.

the tomb, articulate, will record your doing;
I will record it also, this is not art.
this is a kind of science, a kind of hobby,
a kind of personal vice like coin collecting.

it has something to do with horses
and signet rings and school trophies;
it has something to do with the pride of the loins;
it has something to do with good food and music,
and something to do with power, and dancing.
you cannot do this to them, these are my people.

160

Anthem For Doomed Youth

WILFRED OWEN

What passing-bells for these who die as cattle?
      Only the monstrous anger of the guns.
      Only the stuttering rifles' rapid rattle
Can patter out their hasty orisons.
No mockeries now for them; no prayers nor bells,
      Nor any voice of mourning save the choirs, –
The shrill, demented choirs of wailing shells;
      And bugles calling for them from sad shires.

What candles may be held to speed them all?
      Not in the hands of boys, but in their eyes
Shall shine the holy glimmers of good-byes.
      The pallor of girls' brows shall be their pall;
Their flowers the tenderness of patient minds,
And each slow dusk a drawing-down of blinds.

passing-bells] funeral bells rung in churches
orisons] prayers
shires] counties
pall] the cloth draped over a coffin

161

My Dreams Are Of A Field Afar

A.E. HOUSMAN

My dreams are of a field afar
    And blood and smoke and shot.
There in their graves my comrades are,
    In my grave I am not.

I too was taught the trade of man
    And spelt the lesson plain;
But they, when I forgot and ran,
    Remembered and remain.

162

Friend

HONE TUWHARE

Do you remember
that wild stretch of land
with the lone tree guarding the point
from the sharp-tongued sea?

The fort we built out of branches
wrenched from the tree, is dead wood now.
The air that was thick with the whirr of
toetoe spears succumbs at last to the grey gull's wheel.

Oyster-studded roots
of the mangrove yield no finer feast
of silver-bellied eels, and sea-snails
cooked in a rusty can.

Allow me to mend the broken ends
of shared days:
but I wanted to say
that the tree we climbed
that gave food and drink
to youthful dreams, is no more.
Pursed to the lips her fine-edged
leaves made whistle – now stamp
no silken tracery on the cracked
clay floor.

toetoe] tall reed-like grass
tracery] elaborate pattern

Friend,
in this drear
dreamless time I clasp
your hand if only for reassurance
that all our jewelled fantasies were
real and wore splendid rags.

Perhaps the tree
will strike fresh roots again:
give soothing shade to a hurt and
troubled world.

163

A Man I Am

STEVIE SMITH

I was consumed by so much hate
I did not feel that I could wait,
I could not wait for long at anyrate.
I ran into the the forest wild,
I seized a little new born child,
I tore his throat, I licked my fang,
Just like a wolf. A wolf I am.

I ran wild for centuries
Beneath the immemorial trees,
Sometimes I thought my heart would freeze,
And never know a moment's ease,
But presently the spring broke in
Upon the pastures of my sin,
My poor heart bled like anything.
The drops fell down, I knew remorse,
I tasted that primordial curse,
And falling ill, I soon grew worse.
Until at last I cried on Him,
Before whom angel faces dim,
To take the burden of my sin
And break my head beneath his wing.

Upon the silt of death I swam
And as I wept my joy began
Just like a man. A man I am.

primordial] primeval, original

164

Here

R.S. THOMAS

I am a man now.
Pass your hand over my brow,
You can feel the place where the brains grow.

I am like a tree,
From my top boughs I can see
The footprints that led up to me.

There is blood in my veins
That has run clear of the stain
Contracted in so many loins.

Why, then, are my hands red
With the blood of so many dead?
Is this where I was misled?

Why are my hands this way
That they will not do as I say?
Does no God hear when I pray?

I have nowhere to go.
The swift satellites show
The clock of my whole being is slow.

It is too late to start
For destinations not of the heart.
I must stay here with my hurt.

165

A Dream

WILLIAM ALLINGHAM

I heard the dogs howl in the moonlight night;
I went to the window to see the sight;
All the Dead that ever I knew
Going one by one and two by two.

On they passed, and on they passed;
Townsfellows all, from first to last;
Born in the moonlight of the lane,
Quenched in the heavy shadow again.

Schoolmates, marching as when we played
At soldiers once – but now more staid;
Those were the strangest sight to me
Who were drowned, I knew, in the awful sea.

Straight and handsome folk; bent and weak too;
Some that I loved, and gasped to speak to;
Some but a day in their churchyard bed;
Some that I had not known were dead.

A long, long crowd – where each seemed lonely,
Yet of them all there was one, one only,
Raised a head or looked my way:
She lingered a moment, – she might not stay.

How long since I saw that fair pale face!
Ah! Mother dear! might I only place
My head on thy breast, a moment to rest,
While thy hand on my tearful cheek were pressed!

On, on, a moving bridge they made
Across the moon-stream, from shade to shade,
Young and old, women and men;
Many long-forgot, but remembered then.

And first there came a bitter laughter;
A sound of tears the moment after;
And then a music so lofty and gay,
That every morning, day by day,
 I strive to recall it if I may.

166

Time's Fool

RUTH PITTER

Time's fool, but not heaven's: yet hope not for any return.
The rabbit-eaten dry branch and the halfpenny candle
Are lost with the other treasure: the sooty kettle
Thrown away, become redbreast's home in the hedge, where the nettle
Shoots up, and bad bindweed wreathes rust-fretted handle.
Under that broken thing no more shall the dry branch burn.

Poor comfort all comfort: once what the mouse had spared
Was enough, was delight, there where the heart was at home;
The hard cankered apple holed by the wasp and the bird,
The damp bed, with the beetle's tap in the headboard heard,
The dim bit of mirror, three inches of comb:
Dear enough, when with youth and with fancy shared.

I knew that the roots were creeping under the floor,
That the toad was safe in his hole, the poor cat by the fire,
The starling snug in the roof, each slept in his place:
The lily in splendour, the vine in her grace,
The fox in the forest, all had their desire,
As then I had mine, in the place that was happy and poor.

redbreast] robin (bird)
bindweed] a weed common in hedges and fields

167

Cold In The Earth

EMILY BRONTË

Cold in the earth, and the deep snow piled above thee!
Far, far removed, cold in the dreary grave!
Have I forgot, my Only Love, to love thee,
Severed at last by Time's all-wearing wave?

Now, when alone, do my thoughts no longer hover
Over the mountains on Angora's shore;
Resting their wings where heath and fern-leaves cover
That noble heart for ever, ever more?

Cold in the earth, and fifteen wild Decembers
From those brown hills have melted into spring –
Faithful indeed is the spirit that remembers
After such years of change and suffering!

Sweet Love of youth, forgive if I forget thee
While the World's tide is bearing me along:
Sterner desires and darker hopes beset me,
Hopes which obscure but cannot do thee wrong.

No other Sun has lightened up my heaven;
No other Star has ever shone for me:
All my life's bliss from thy dear life was given –
All my life's bliss is in the grave with thee.

But when the days of golden dreams had perished
And even Despair was powerless to destroy,
Then did I learn how existence could be cherished,
Strengthened and fed without the aid of joy;

all-wearing] i.e. which wears everything away

Then did I check the tears of useless passion,
Weaned my young soul from yearning after thine;
Sternly denied its burning wish to hasten
Down to that tomb already more than mine!

And even yet, I dare not let it languish,
Dare not indulge in Memory's rapturous pain;
Once drinking deep of that divinest anguish,
How could I seek the empty world again?

168

A Quoi Bon Dire

CHARLOTTE MEW

Seventeen years ago you said
    Something that sounded like Good-bye;
    And everybody thinks that you are dead,
      But I.

    So I, as I grow stiff and cold
To this and that say Good-bye too;
    And everybody sees that I am old
      But you.

    And one fine morning in a sunny lane
Some boy and girl will meet and kiss and swear
    That nobody can love their way again
      While over there
You will have smiled, I shall have tossed your hair.

A Quoi Bon Dire] (French) what's the good/what's the point

169

From *The Triumph of Time*

A.C. SWINBURNE

Before our lives divide for ever,
    While time is with us and hands are free,
(Time, swift to fasten and swift to sever
    Hand from hand, as we stand by the sea)
I will say no word that a man might say
Whose whole life's love goes down in a day;
For this could never have been; and never,
    Though the gods and the years relent, shall be.

Is it worth a tear, is it worth an hour,
    To think of things that are well outworn?
Of fruitless husk and fugitive flower,
    The dream foregone and the deed forborne?
Though joy be done with and grief be vain,
Time shall not sever us wholly in twain;
Earth is not spoilt for a single shower;
    But the rain has ruined the ungrown corn.

It will grow not again, this fruit of my heart,
    Smitten with sunbeams, ruined with rain.
The singing seasons divide and depart,
    Winter and summer depart in twain.
It will grow not again, it is ruined at root,
The bloodlike blossom, the dull red fruit;
Though the heart yet sickens, the lips yet smart,
    With sullen savour of poisonous pain.

twain] two
sullen savour] sour taste

I have given no man of my fruit to eat;
        I trod the grapes, I have drunken the wine.
Had you eaten and drunken and found it sweet,
        This wild new growth of the corn and vine,
This wine and bread without lees or leaven,
We had grown as gods, as the gods in heaven,
Souls fair to look upon, goodly to greet,
        One splendid spirit, your soul and mine.

In the change of years, in the coil of things,
        In the clamour and rumour of life to be,
We, drinking love at the furthest springs,
        Covered with love as a covering tree,
We had grown as gods, as the gods above,
Filled from the heart to the lips with love,
Held fast in his hands, clothed warm with his wings,
        O love, my love, had you loved but me!

We had stood as the sure stars stand, and moved
        As the moon moves, loving the world; and seen
Grief collapse as a thing disproved,
        Death consume as a thing unclean.
Twain halves of a perfect heart, made fast
Soul to soul while the years fell past;
Had you loved me once, as you have not loved;
        Had the chance been with us that has not been.

lees] sediment in wine
leaven] yeast
coil] turmoil

170

Meeting At Night

ROBERT BROWNING

The grey sea and the long black land;
And the yellow half-moon large and low;
And the startled little waves that leap
In fiery ringlets from their sleep,
As I gain the cove with pushing prow,
And quench its speed i' the slushy sand.

Then a mile of warm sea-scented beach;
Three fields to cross till a farm appears;
A tap at the pane, the quick sharp scratch
And blue spurt of a lighted match,
And a voice less loud, through its joys and fears,
Than the two hearts beating each to each!

prow] the front part of a boat

171

Because I Liked You Better

A.E. HOUSMAN

Because I liked you better
    Than suits a man to say,
It irked you, and I promised
    To throw the thought away.

To put the world between us
    We parted, stiff and dry;
'Good-bye', said you, 'forget me.'
    'I will, no fear', said I.

If here, where clover whitens
    The dead man's knoll, you pass,
And no tall flower to meet you
    Starts in the trefoiled grass,

Halt by the headstone naming
    The heart no longer stirred,
And say the lad that loved you
    Was one that kept his word.

knoll] hillock, mound
trefoiled grass] i.e. clover

172

From *The Ballad of Reading Gaol*

OSCAR WILDE

He did not wear his scarlet coat,
    For blood and wine are red,
And blood and wine were on his hands
    When they found him with the dead,
The poor dead woman whom he loved,
    And murdered in her bed.

He walked amongst the Trial Men
    In a suit of shabby grey;
A cricket cap was on his head,
    And his step seemed light and gay;
But I never saw a man who looked
    So wistfully at the day.

I never saw a man who looked
    With such a wistful eye
Upon that little tent of blue
    Which prisoners call the sky,
And at every drifting cloud that went
    With sails of silver by.

I walked, with other souls in pain,
    Within another ring,
And was wondering if the man had done
    A great or little thing,
When a voice behind me whispered low,
    'That fellow's got to swing.'

scarlet coat] soldier's tunic
Trial Men] i.e. those in the courtroom
swing] hang

Dear Christ! the very prison walls
    Suddenly seemed to reel,
And the sky above my head became
    Like a casque of scorching steel;
And, though I was a soul in pain,
    My pain I could not feel.

I only knew what hunted thought
    Quickened his step, and why
He looked upon the garish day
    With such a wistful eye;
The man had killed the thing he loved,
    And so he had to die.

       · · · · ·

Yet each man kills the thing he loves,
    By each let this be heard,
Some do it with a bitter look,
    Some with a flattering word,
The coward does it with a kiss,
    The brave man with a sword!

Some kill their love when they are young,
    And some when they are old;
Some strangle with the hands of Lust,
    Some with the hands of Gold:
The kindest use a knife, because
    The dead so soon grow cold.

Some love too little, some too long,
    Some sell, and others buy;
Some do the deed with many tears,
    And some without a sigh:
For each man kills the thing he loves,
    Yet each man does not die.

He does not die a death of shame
    On a day of dark disgrace,
Nor have a noose about his neck,
    Nor a cloth upon his face,
Nor drop feet foremost through the floor
    Into an empty space.

casque] helmet

Index of First Lines

A chimney-sweeper's boy am I   92
A cool small evening shrunk to a dog bark and the clank   149
A free bird leaps   115
A little black thing among the snow   94
A married state affords but little ease   69
Adieu, farewell, earth's bliss   16
Ants prudent bite the ends of hoarded wheat   51
As I sat at the Café I said to myself   123
As loving hind that, hartless, wants her deer   67
As waked from sleep, methought I heard the voice   74
'As you came from the holy land   23
Ask me no more where Jove bestows   22
At dawn the ridge emerges massed and dun   223
At the instant of drowning he invoked the three sisters   142
Away, melancholy   202

Be judge yourself, I'll bring it to the test   90
Because I could not stop for Death   208
Because I liked you better   242
Before our lives divide for ever   239
Betwixt two ridges of ploughed land lay Wat   86
Blow, blow, thou winter wind   34
By this he knew she wept with waking eyes   189

Cold in the earth, and the deep snow piled above thee!   236
Cold was the night wind, drifting fast the snows fell   78
Come, darkest night, becoming sorrow best   18
Come live with me, and be my love   27
Cruising these residential Sunday   172

Death, be not proud, though some have called thee   104
Distinguish carefully between these two   126
Do you remember   229
Drink to me only with thine eyes   40

Earth has not anything to show more fair   177
Even such is time, which takes in trust   15

False life! a foil and no more, when   102
Fear no more the heat o' th' sun   20
For the green turtle with her pulsing burden   150
Full fathom five thy father lies   42

Gather ye rosebuds while ye may   55
Glory be to God for dappled things   162
Go, lovely rose!   11
Golden slumbers kiss your eyes   41
Good reader, now you tasted have   43
Great Pan is not dead   161

Happy insect, what can be   53
Happy the man whose wish and care   70
He did not wear his scarlet coat   243
He knew in the hour he died   216
He never learned her, quite. Year after year   155
Here first the day does break   63
How do I love thee? Let me count the ways!   157

I am a man now   232
I am content, I do not care   96
I am the nor'west air nosing among the pines   145
I am the poet of the Body and I am the poet of the Soul   192
I feed a flame within which so torments me   61
I grieve, and dare not show my discontent   39
I hate that drum's discordant sound   83
I have had playmates, I have had companions   137
I have thought so much about the girl   129
I heard the dogs howl in the moonlight night   233
I like working near a door. I like to have my work-bench   124
I met a traveller from an antique land   201
I ne'er was struck before that hour   154
I sat all morning in the college sick bay   138
I struck the board, and cried, 'No more'   100
I used to think that grown-up people chose   207
I wake up cold, I who   181
I was consumed by so much hate   231
I watched a giant cockroach start to pace   171
If the year is meditating a suitable gift   199
'I'm rising five', he said   117
In unexperienced infancy   48
In Xanadu did Kubla Khan   110

Intense blue morning   127
Is the fish ready? You're a tedious while   71
'Is there anybody there?' said the Traveller   139
It is not growing like a tree   19

Know then thyself, presume not God to scan;   112

Little Fly   47
Love in fantastic triumph sat   60
Love's an headstrong wild desire   58

Men of England, wherefore plough   121
My dreams are of a field afar   228
My father worked with a horse-plough   215
My heart is like a singing bird   169
My parents kept me from children who were rough   211
My prime of youth is but a frost of cares   14

Nights like this: on the cold apple-bough   148
No crookèd leg, no blearèd eye   12
Nobody heard him, the dead man   141
Now from each van   84
Now that the world is all in amaze   95

Of this world's theatre in which we stay   28
On the road to the bay was a lake of rushes   178
One day I wrote her name upon the strand   30
One man shall smile one day and say goodbye   222

People are made of places. They carry with them   176
Pike, three inches long, perfect   167
Pity me not because the light of day   158

Rain, midnight rain, nothing but the wild rain   183
Romira, stay   56

Seventeen years ago you said   238
Shall I compare thee to a summer's day?   32
She dwelt among the untrodden ways   130
she sat down   134
Sigh no more, ladies, sigh no more   6
Since there's no help, come let us kiss and part   10
So forth issued the seasons of the year   35

So we must part, my body, you and I   184
So, we'll go no more a-roving   156
Some hand, that never meant to do thee hurt   200
Spring, the sweet spring, is the year's pleasant king   31
Stand on the highest pavement of the stair   191
Stop all the clocks, cut off the telephone   190
Straws like tame lightnings lie about the grass   175
Sun-warmed in this late season's grace   166
Sundays too my father got up early   136
Sweet are the thoughts that savour of content   38

Tears, idle tears, I know not what they mean   210
Tell me not, sweet, I am unkind   82
That time of year thou mayst in me behold   33
The art of losing isn't hard to master   209
The children are at the loom of another world   120
The curfew tolls the knell of parting day   105
The flower-fed buffaloes of the spring   152
The flowers that on the banks and walks did grow   25
The glories of our blood and state   103
The grey sea and the long black land   241
The man of life upright   37
The moon rolls over the roof and falls behind   163
The name of the product I tested is *Life*   197
The poetry of earth is never dead   151
The sea is calm to-night   146
The spirit is too blunt an instrument   186
The trees are coming into leaf   220
The wind flapped loose, the wind was still   170
These emmets, how little they are in our eyes!   52
They are cutting down the great plane-trees at the end of the garden   218
They asked me 'Are you sitting down?   195
They flee from me, that sometime did me seek   9
They plan. They build. All spaces are gridded   174
Those lumbering horses in the steady plough   164
Though my mother was already two years dead   188
Time again for the annual joust, the regular fanfare   224
Time's fool, but not heaven's: yet hope not for any return   235
Tuckett. Bill Tuckett. Telegraph operator, Hall's Creek   180
'Twas at the silent, solemn hour   75

Weep you no more, sad fountains   7
Well, World, you have kept faith with me   194

What does he do with them all, the old king   143
What is our life? A play of passion   29
What passing-bells for these who die as cattle?   227
What thing is love? – for sure love is a thing   4
When I consider how my light is spent   99
When I was fair and young, and favour graced me   8
When I was young and there were five of us   132
When you dyed your hair blue   212
Where lies the land to which the ship would go?   179
Why do I love? Go, ask the glorious sun   65
Why so pale and wan, fond lover?   3
With how sad steps, O Moon, thou climb'st the skies!   13
Woman much missed, how you call to me, call to me   144
Work-table, litter, books and standing lamp   182

Ye living lamps, by whose dear light   62
Yes, injured Woman! rise, assert thy right!   80
You endless torments that my rest oppress   5
You know the school; you call it old   221
You should be here, Nature has need of you   153
You were   214
You will see him light a cigarette   131
you cannot do this to them, these are my people   226
Your mouth contorting in brief spite and   119